Basic Accounting for Community Organizations and Small Groups

DATE DUE

Praise for this book

'*Basic Accounting for Community Organizations and Small Groups* is much needed for the NGO sector. Many organizations are small and therefore this book fills their need. It is written in a simple manner from a layperson's perspective, and will be very useful. This book can be summarized as "the power of keeping things simple".'

Sanjay Patra, Executive Director,
Financial Management Service Foundation, India

'John Cammack says that one of the key qualities of a book-keeper or treasurer for a community organization is being "able to explain financial matters to those who have less experience". John does just that in this book. He sets out clearly how anyone, whether they have previous experience of finance or not, can follow simple steps to keep good accounts. This book shows that managing money well can be simple and is possible for everyone and every group.'

Tim Boyes-Watson, Director of Mango
(Management Accounting for NGOs)

'John Cammack has a unique talent of being able to explain complex accounting in an engaging and accessible manner. This is another invaluable tool for small organizations that are striving to achieve good financial management.'

Neil Jennings, Founder of Accounting for
International Development

Basic Accounting for Community Organizations and Small Groups

A practical guide

John Cammack

PRACTICAL ACTION
Publishing

Practical Action Publishing Ltd
The Schumacher Centre
Bourton on Dunsmore, Rugby,
Warwickshire CV23 9QZ, UK
www.practicalactionpublishing.org

ISBN 978-1-85339-820-9 Hardback
ISBN 978-1-85339-821-6 Paperback
ISBN 978-1-78044-820-6 Library Ebook
ISBN 978-1-78044-821-3 Ebook

Cammack, J. (2014) *Basic Accounting for Community Organizations and Small Groups: A Practical Guide*, Rugby, UK: Practical Action Publishing <http://dx.doi.org/10.3362/9781780448206>.

Since 1974, Practical Action Publishing has published and disseminated books and information in support of international development work throughout the world. Practical Action Publishing is a trading name of Practical Action Publishing Ltd (Company Reg. No. 1159018), the wholly owned publishing company of Practical Action. Practical Action Publishing trades only in support of its parent charity objectives and any profits are covenanted back to Practical Action (Charity Reg. No. 247257, Group VAT Registration No. 880 9924 76).

Cover illustration: © Martha Hardy@GCI
Typeset by SJI Services, New Delhi
Printed in the United Kingdom

Contents

http://dx.doi.org/10.3362/9781780448206.000

Acknowledgements

Thanks are due to many people who have helped directly or indirectly in the production of this book. I am grateful to those who read through the earlier drafts: Freda Cammack, Stephen Cammack, and Gopal Rao; and staff of Practical Action Publishing: Toby Milner, Clare Tawney and Kelly Somers. Thanks also to proofreader Kim Daniel and to Martha Hardy for the cover illustration.

I also acknowledge those who helped me develop the material in earlier editions: Alison Beaumont, Peter Howlett, Jacques Laurol, Terry Lewis, Stephen Lloyd, Catherine Robinson, and staff from Oxfam international country offices.

Many people who have participated in training events which I have facilitated have helped me, often unknowingly, to develop the material and my own understanding of the way in which people learn. I thank them too.

Special thanks are due to Freda and Stephen, who have been a support throughout the time of writing.

John Cammack
Oxford, 2014

About the author

John Cammack works as an adviser and consultant, trainer, writer, and coach in the non-government organization (NGO) sector. He was head of international finance at Oxfam GB and senior lecturer in accounting and financial management at Oxford Brookes University. He now works with a range of international development and relief agencies. His website is www.johncammack.net.

His consultancy work includes: financial management and programme management reviews and capacity building for European and Southern-based organizations, working with NGOs and community-based organizations, and advising organizations on becoming 'fit for funding'. His participatory training includes: building non-profit financial capacity, financial management for non-specialists, training trainers (and specialist courses for training financial trainers), and developing communication between finance and non-finance staff working internationally and cross-culturally.

He is the author of *Communicating Financial Management with Non-finance People* (Practical Action Publishing), *Building Financial Management Capacity for NGOs and Community Organizations* (Practical Action Publishing), and *Financial Management for Development* (Intrac). He co-authored *Financial Management for Emergencies* (www.fme-online.org). John is a professionally qualified accountant, manager, and teacher and specializes in the international not-for-profit sector. He holds an MSc in International Development Management, and an MBA.

Glossary

Accountant Someone who is qualified (usually by passing professional examinations) to give financial advice (see Chapter 1)

Accounting The method of recording and using information to prepare financial summaries/statements and reports (see Chapter 1)

Accounts The records kept and statements produced to show how a group has used its money (see Chapter 1)

Analysed cash and bank book The record of all cash and/or bank amounts coming in and going out, with additional columns to identify the type of receipt or payment (see Chapter 4)

Audit An independent assessment of a group's accounts and other records (see Chapter 10)

Auditor A person who carries out an audit (see Chapter 10)

Audit report A written document signed by the examiner/auditor, which is attached to the receipts and payments account at the year-end (see Chapter 10)

Bank book A record kept by the group itself, showing all items going in or out of the bank account (see Chapter 5)

Bank charge A charge made for operating a bank account (see Chapter 6)

Bank pass book A book provided and updated by the bank to show the record of money in an account (see Chapter 6)

Bank paying-in book see *Paying-in book*

Bank reconciliation A way of confirming that a group's own accounting records agree with those of the bank (see Chapter 6)

Bank statement A list produced by a bank, showing all entries in an account over a period of time, and the balance held at the end of that period (see Chapter 6)

Book-keeper A person who keeps records of accounts (see Chapter 1)

Budget A financial summary of a plan relating to a period of time (see Chapter 2)

Budget and actual statement A report comparing budget and actual receipts and payments (see Chapter 9)

Cash book A record of all cash coming in and going out. The term is also used to mean the cash *and* bank book records (see Chapter 3)

Cash-flow forecast (or cash budget) A way of stating, in advance, what money is expected to come in and go out of a group or project over a fixed period of time (see Chapter 2)

Cheque A document provided by a bank to enable you to withdraw money from your bank account (see Chapter 5)

Cheque (or check) account See *Current account*

Closing balance A figure included in the accounts as an amount remaining at the end of an accounting period. This will be the same as the opening balance in the next period (see Chapter 3)

Contract (with donor) See *Letter of agreement*

Cumulative budget and actual report A statement comparing budgeted and actual receipts and payments from the beginning of the year to date

Cumulative total The total for the current period added to the total for previous periods (see Chapter 9)

Current account A type of bank account into which money can be paid, and from which cheques can be written and money withdrawn (see Chapter 5)

Deposit account A bank account that gains interest. The bank may require several days' advance notice to withdraw funds. Sometimes called a savings account (see Chapter 5)

Donor An individual or organization providing financial support or other forms of support to a group (see Chapter 11)

Examination An independent assessment of a group's accounts and other records (see Chapter 10). Also called 'independent examination', 'independent review', 'an inspection', or simply 'an audit' because it is difficult to tell the difference

Examiner An independent person responsible for assessing the accounts at the year-end (see Chapter 10). Also called 'independent examiner' or 'independent reviewer'

Expenditure (or expenses) Costs which have been paid (see Chapter 2)

Fixed assets Items which are kept for more than one year, for example vehicles and equipment (see Chapter 8)

Group Used to mean a community organization or small group

Income receipt A piece of paper that gives details of an amount of money received, and the signature of the person receiving the money (see Chapter 3)

Independent examination/review See *Examination*

Independent examiner/reviewer See *Examiner*

Inflation A term used to refer to an increase in prices (see Chapter 2)

Interest An amount added to your money when someone else holds it – for example, a bank – or an amount charged on a bank overdraft (see Chapter 5)

Invoice A written request for payment (see Chapter 3)

Letter of agreement An agreement between a donor and a group, setting out terms and conditions for the relationship (see Chapter 11)

Management committee Volunteers who are (legally) responsible for the running of a group (see Chapter 1). Also called 'governing body', 'trustees', 'board', 'management board', 'executive committee' or simply 'the committee'

Management letter A summary of findings and recommendations sent to the group's leader or management committee at the end of an examination of the accounts or (especially) a formal audit (see Chapter 10)

Objectives A summary of future plans (see Chapter 2)

Opening balance An amount of money which is included in the cash book, bank book, or other record as a starting point at the beginning of a new accounting period (see Chapter 3)

Overdraft An amount that a bank allows to be temporarily overspent from your account. It is, in effect, a short-term loan (see Chapter 5)

Paying-in book/slip A document provided by a bank which you complete when you pay money into your current account (see Chapter 5)

Payment Money given to someone else for the provision of goods or services (see Chapter 2)

Payment receipt A piece of paper that shows an amount paid and the signature of the person who has received the money (see Chapter 3)

Receipt Money coming in; or a piece of paper acknowledging money received or payment made (see Chapter 3)

Receipts and payments account A summary of bank and cash items coming in and going out of a group over a period of time (see Chapter 7)

Reconciliation A way of agreeing one part of the accounts with another (see Chapter 6). See *Bank reconciliation*

Savings account A bank account which pays interest and is intended for money that is not required immediately; may also be called a deposit account (see Chapter 5)

Treasurer The person who keeps records of the accounts and interprets their meaning to others in the group (see Chapter 1)

Voucher A receipt for money; or a document which supports a financial transaction; for example, an invoice (see Chapter 3)

Preface

The thought of taking on the responsibility for keeping accounting records fills many people with horror. 'What does it all mean?' 'What do I do with all these figures?' and 'Where do I start?' are common reactions. But proper financial control can be key to the success of an activity or group, whatever its size, and the basic principles – being logical and consistent – are not difficult to apply, once they have been explained.

If you are running a small group or project without any experience of keeping accounts, this book is for you. It should help you to understand the basic rules and put them into practice with confidence. More detailed accounting information will be needed in some cases, if (for example) you need to calculate profits in a trading operation. Such information is beyond the scope of this book; but if you have no other help, at least the system explained here will keep your records in order. Places to go for additional help are shown in the Written and Web resources.

This book builds on *Basic Accounting for Small Groups* published in 1992 and 2003. It includes questions and activities (together with solutions) to give you a chance to practise. This is intended to build your confidence with a case study before moving on to your own accounting records.

The book also includes notes on the activities to help trainers and facilitators. Some of the activities in this book are available to download from the Practical Action Publishing website.

No currency has been quoted in any of the examples in the book, because (we hope) it will be used in different countries. Amounts are shown in the text with zeros after the decimal point, for example 20.00. Technical terms are printed in bold in the text and are explained in the Glossary.

This book is the result of many years' experience of giving advice on financial systems with international development groups and community organizations. The procedures which the book describes, however, are not specific to development programmes. It is hoped that it will be useful to any small group that needs to keep accurate records of its financial transactions.

Use of the activities at the end of each chapter

This book is based around two fictitious case studies – the first *Primary Health-care Programme* in the main text; and the second *Training for Development,* on which the activities are based.

The practical activities will be found at the end of each chapter. Their purpose is to build your confidence in keeping basic accounts in an imaginary context and to develop skills which can then be used in a real organization.

The length of these activities varies; you may be able to complete some of them in one session, for others you may need longer. Some of the activities are designed to go a little further than the text and encourage you to think through what the information means and how it might be used.

You will find the solutions to the activities in Appendix C. Although it is tempting to check whether you have the right approach, it is probably better to attempt the question before referring to the solution!

The book aims, by itself, to provide enough help for a person without formal qualifications to be able to maintain a basic accounting system. However, if you are doing the activities on your own, you may find it helpful to ask a friend or a colleague who has some experience of financial record keeping to act as your mentor or adviser. Such a person may increase your motivation to complete the activities, and help you, if you wish, to go further than the scope of this book allows.

CHAPTER 1

Introduction: why keep accounts – and who should keep them?

This chapter shows why it is necessary to keep accounts for community organizations and small groups and who should keep them. It considers the qualities that a book-keeper, accountant or treasurer responsible for the accounting should have, and their relationship with an organization or group and its management committee. It lists some of the duties required, the reasons why a group needs to keep clear accounting information, and the benefits of doing so.

Keywords: qualities of book-keeper, accountant or treasurer; basic accounting for community organizations; basic accounting for small groups

Clear accounting maintains friendship. (Nicaraguan proverb)

Why keep accounts?

All community organizations and small groups need clear **accounting**, for a number of reasons:

- All members of the group need to know what money is available and how money has been spent.
- Accounting is often required by law.
- Donors – the people who have given money to the group – need to know how their funds have been used.

http://dx.doi.org/10.3362/9781780448206.001

- The information provided by clear accounts helps to run the group.
- It 'maintains friendship', by showing that the person responsible for keeping the accounts is honest.

The aim of this book is to help you to maintain records of money coming in and going out; to show you how to make use of the information provided; and to show how to prepare a summary of the way in which the money has been used.

Who keeps accounts?

It is usual for a group to appoint one person to take a leading role in looking after financial information. This could be a paid **book-keeper** or **accountant.** Sometimes a member of the group will do this work voluntarily. Such a person is often called the **treasurer.**

The paid person or the voluntary treasurer will help members of the group to plan what they want to do with the available funds. Other duties include keeping accurate accounting records, preparing summaries of how money has been spent and arranging for an independent person to check the accounts once a year. They will deal with the bank and arrange the payments of salaries and bills.

However, it is the responsibility of the entire group – or a **management committee** on its behalf – and any staff to make sure that the accounting is in good order and that they understand the information presented by the book-keeper, accountant or treasurer. The group (or its committee) may rely on this person for technical information but everyone is responsible for sound financial management. This is because the money belongs to the group and to the people who have donated it.

What qualities should a book-keeper, accountant or treasurer have?

If someone is paid to keep the accounting records they may already have some experience which they can use to help the group set up the standard records. Sometimes the person appointed has little accounting experience, although they may have a lot of general experience. This book would help both to set up accounting records.

If someone is paid, the group may still appoint a voluntary treasurer from their own members; in small groups the treasurer might do all the work. It is beneficial if a group appoints a treasurer who has some previous accounting experience. This is not always possible, but if you work your way through this book you will understand the basic requirements for keeping accounts in good order.

The following are some of the qualities required in a paid person or voluntary treasurer. He or she should be:

- honest, and seen to be honest;
- methodical;
- able to keep accurate records;
- confident in dealing with money;
- confident in communicating with employees of a bank and other organizations;
- able to explain financial matters to people who have less experience.

It may be possible to give support to the treasurer if he or she is not confident to do all the technical tasks of accounting. Someone from outside the group may be able to provide this help, for example an accountant. Such a person may require payment for this service.

Activities for Chapter 1 *solutions in Appendix C*

1.1 List five reasons why groups need to keep accounting
information.

a.

b.

c.

d.

e.

1.2 Mark each of your answers in 1.1 with the letter 'L' if the
reason is required by the law or an outside organization,
or with an 'I' if it is needed for the group's internal
purposes.

1.3 Name six qualities required for a person who is acting
as book-keeper, accountant or treasurer.

a.

b.

c.

d.

e.

f.

1.4 Answer the following questions:

a. What tasks would you expect a book-keeper,
accountant or treasurer to do?

b. For each task listed in 1.4a, decide whether the level of
skill required is high (**H**), medium (**M**), or low (**L**). If a
treasurer does not have the skills required to complete
all the high-level tasks, what could be done?

c. Does anyone other than the paid person or voluntary
treasurer of a group need to be concerned about the
accounts? If so, who? And why?

CHAPTER 2

Deciding what your group's activities will cost

The first stage in keeping accounts comes before any money has been spent. It is the stage when you decide what you want to do, and how much it will cost, often described as 'budgeting'. This chapter takes you through planning budgeting objectives, constructing a budget, and breaking down the budget to decide how much money will come in and go out each month. It considers how to treat price increases (or 'inflation') when preparing the budget and how to build in amounts to cover this. It starts to look at case study examples of a group and provides activities to help you practise preparing the documents shown.

Keywords: budgeting objectives; budgets; budgets and price increases; cash-flow forecasts; example of a budget

Before anything else you need to plan what the group would like to do and work out the cost.

Establishing your plans

Firstly, you need to decide your **objectives** – that is to say, what you want to achieve – and secondly how your activities will help achieve these objectives. This is not something that the person responsible for the accounts can do alone. As far as possible, every member of the group needs to be involved

http://dx.doi.org/10.3362/9781780448206.002

in the discussion, so that they will feel committed to what happens.

The next stage should also be discussed with the entire group. This is to decide what is needed in order to achieve these objectives; for example:

- How many people will be needed?
- Will they need to travel?
- What materials are required?
- Will premises be needed?

You should then find out what these items will cost. Some of these costs will be more obvious than others. Sometimes you will need to talk with merchants or suppliers to obtain estimates of the cost of materials. You should choose the most appropriate estimate (which will not necessarily be the lowest).

After you have gathered together all the information about costs, you need to write them down on paper, item by item. It is important at this stage to make sure that each type of cost is written down separately, as shown in Figure 1. This listing is called a **budget**.

How to construct a budget

The budget should be for a fixed period of time; for example, one year. In the examples used in this book, the financial year (January to December) is the same as the calendar year. This is not always the case.

The budget should include not only details of costs (also called **payments**, **expenses**, or **expenditure**), but also money that you know (or are fairly certain) you will receive. When you apply to donors for money, you will need to give them your proposed budget, excluding the amount of money you hope they will give you.

Budgets usually include detailed calculations, for example 12 months' salary at 400.00 per month plus employer tax and benefits of 360.00.

Let's look at an example of a budget. Figure 1 relates to a primary health-care programme, but the same rules apply to all budgets.

Figure 1 Example of a budget

Primary Health-care Programme budget for the period 1 January to 31 December 20--	
Money coming in	
Grant from donor (note 1)	19,000
Grant from Department of Health (note 1)	28,000
Miscellaneous sales (note 2)	600
Total	**47,600**
Money going out	
Salaries (note 3)	12,000
Rent of premises (note 4)	5,000
Purchase of drugs (note 5)	10,000
Medical supplies (note 6)	17,600
Electricity (note 7)	1,000
Office expenses (note 8)	2,000
Total	**47,600**

Notes
1. Funding is confirmed for both grants.
2. Miscellaneous sales: drugs and medical supplies for 12 months at 50.00 per month.
3. Salaries: Medical Director: 12 months' salary at 400.00 per month, plus employer tax and benefits of 360.00 per year. Nurse and Administrator 12 months' salary at 260.00 per month x 2, plus employer tax and benefits of 300.00 per year x 2.
4. Fixed contract for one year's rent.
5. Drugs: two purchases of 5,000.00 each, based on a detailed breakdown prepared by the Medical Director.
6. Medical supplies: four purchases of 4,400.00 each based on a detailed breakdown prepared by the Medical Director.
7. Electricity: based on current year's consumption plus projected increase of 5 per cent.
8. Annual insurance of 170.00 and audit fee of 150.00 for the year. Postage (20.00), telephone (50.00), stationery (20.00), and travel costs (50.00), a total of 140.00 per month.

When you apply for money from a donor, you will need to submit your proposed budget. In Figure 1, two grants are included. This would indicate that these donors have already agreed to fund the programme. Copies of the detailed breakdown for drugs and medical supplies, notes 5 and 6, should be attached to the budget.

We will go through Figure 1 item by item to see how the budget was made:

Grants. This budget assumes that the grants have already been agreed. There may be a stage before this when, for example, the Department of Health has definitely promised a grant, but the grant from the other donor is uncertain. If so, either it should be excluded from the budget, or a note could be written at the side of the item, to say that it is not guaranteed.

Miscellaneous sales. Some drugs or other medical supplies will be sold. It is always difficult to estimate how many sales there will be – particularly with medical programmes, as the demand for drugs and medical supplies is difficult to predict. The only way to estimate sales is to take your best guess, for example by calculating a monthly average, and try not to be too optimistic.

Salaries. Calculate the number of people employed by the group, and the amount paid to them. Remember to include any extra costs, such as insurance, government taxes, and benefits paid by the employer.

Rent of premises. If you have selected a building, the rent can be agreed with the owner. If you have not yet rented a building, find out what a similar one is likely to cost.

Purchase of drugs and medical supplies. For large items such as these, you should ask for written estimates from several suppliers.

Electricity. Ask other people in your area about the local charges for items such as electricity and water.

Office expenses. Although only one amount is included in the budget, in this example it covers a number of different items, such as insurance, audit, post, telephone, stationery, and travel costs. A breakdown of these is shown in the notes to the budget.

Remember that costs may rise from the time when you prepare your budget to the time when you spend the money. Try to allow for this in your calculations.

Breaking down the budget

The next stage of preparing the budget is to decide how much money will come in and go out in each individual month. Figures 2a and 2b give an example of how this breakdown looks, using the information in Figure 1. There are two reasons for presenting the budget in this way:

- It helps you to monitor money coming in and going out month by month. (We will look at this again in Chapter 9.)
- It shows whether you will have enough money coming in to pay for what is going out. There are three sections to this breakdown:
  1. Money coming in, listed by budget item, month by month (Figure 2a).
  2. Money going out, listed by budget item, month by month (Figure 2b).
  3. A summary of the money held at the start, plus the total coming in, less the total going out. This is shown month by month and can be used to show the times of the year when you are likely to run out of money (Figure 3).

In the example in Figure 3, the *Primary Health-care Programme* has 1,000.00 held at 1 January and at the end of December, because the 'money coming in' and 'money going out' are exactly the same (47,600.00).

Figure 2b shows a few of the 'money going out' items as different figures for individual months. This may be because items have different payment dates. 'Office expenses', for example, show a total payment of 2,000.00 for the year: the payment of the insurance premium (170.00) is due in January, and the audit fee (150.00) is due in December, and the other costs are spread evenly at a rate of 140.00 per month.

Figure 2a *Primary Health-care Programme* budget of money coming in, broken down January to December

	JAN	FEB	MAR	APR	MAY	JUN	JUL	AUG	SEP	OCT	NOV	DEC	TOTAL
MONEY COMING IN													
Grant from donor	9,500						9,500						19,000
Grant from Dept of Health	14,000						14,000						28,000
Miscellaneous sales	50	50	50	50	50	50	50	50	50	50	50	50	600
Total [A]	**23,550**	**50**	**50**	**50**	**50**	**50**	**23,550**	**50**	**50**	**50**	**50**	**50**	**47,600**

Figure 2b *Primary Health-care Programme* budget of money going out, broken down January to December

	JAN	FEB	MAR	APR	MAY	JUN	JUL	AUG	SEP	OCT	NOV	DEC	TOTAL
MONEY GOING OUT													
Salaries	1,000	1,000	1,000	1,000	1,000	1,000	1,000	1,000	1,000	1,000	1,000	1,000	12,000
Rent of premises	417	417	417	417	417	417	417	417	416	416	416	416	5,000
Purchase of drugs	5,000					5,000							10,000
Medical supplies	4,400			4,400			4,400			4,400			17,600
Electricity	83	83	83	83	83	83	83	83	84	84	84	84	1,000
Office expenses	310	140	140	140	140	140	140	140	140	140	140	290	2,000
Total [B]	**11,210**	**1,640**	**1,640**	**6,040**	**1,640**	**6,640**	**6,040**	**1,640**	**1,640**	**6,040**	**1,640**	**1,790**	**47,600**

Figure 3 *Primary Health-care Programme* budgeted money available at end of the month, January to December (cash-flow forecast)

	JAN	FEB	MAR	APR	MAY	JUN	JUL	AUG	SEP	OCT	NOV	DEC
Money at start of month [C]	1,000	13,340	11,750	10,160	4,170	2,580	(4,010)	13,500	11,910	10,320	4,330	2,740
Plus total money coming in [A]	23,550	50	50	50	50	50	23,550	50	50	50	50	50
Less total money going out [B]	11,210	1,640	1,640	6,040	1,640	6,640	6,040	1,640	1,640	6,040	1,640	1,790
Money at end of month [C+A–B]	**13,340**	**11,750**	**10,160**	**4,170**	**2,580**	**(4,010)**	**13,500**	**11,910**	**10,320**	**4,330**	**2,740**	**1,000**

Brackets around the figures show that it is a negative amount. The monthly totals of money coming in and going out are identified by the letters [A] and [B] respectively.

Letter [C] is the amount at the beginning of each month. In Figure 3 the amount held at the end of each month becomes the money at the start of the following month.

In the example shown in Figure 3, the month of June (just before more money comes in) is the one when funds are expected to run out. To avoid problems, examine the breakdown carefully to see if you could pay for purchases later than planned, or ask the people giving you grants to pay slightly earlier. If this is not possible, you may need to arrange a temporary loan for the period when you have insufficient money.

A breakdown like the one shown in Figures 2 and 3 will alert you, in advance, to the financial situation, and whether or not you need to do anything about it. This is called a **cash-flow forecast**. The information contained in this document should be updated each month.

Whenever you request funds from a donor or government department, or need a bank loan, it is important to support your request with a budget and cash-flow forecast.

Towards the end of each year, you will need to prepare a budget and cash-flow forecast for the next financial year. When you are preparing a second budget you will, however, have gained valuable experience in what is likely to happen, and how much items cost. You will, for example, know about any monthly variations in expenditure.

You must keep referring back to the budget and cash-flow forecast as the year progresses. Sometimes you will need to revise the figures. If you do, always tell your donors. It is helpful to prepare a budget for one or two years in advance, and donors will sometimes ask for this.

Budgets and price increases

Because budgets are prepared in advance, price increases may affect items in your budget even before you start to spend. This is often referred to as **inflation**. You will be aware from your own personal finances what this means. There are no simple ways to deal with it.

You should build into your budget an amount to cover possible increases. You will have different categories of price increases:

- *Items that are likely to increase in price*: if you do not know what the increase is going to be, the rate of previous changes will give you a guide. There may be a government forecast of how prices will increase. Use this with care, because governments tend to be over-optimistic. It is far better to use your own best estimate.
- *Salaries* are more difficult to estimate, because they will depend on the general level of price increases. Unless you have already agreed on salary increases for the following year, you will have to put your best estimate in the budget. Such a guess can lead to trouble: staff may assume that it will be a reality.
- *Items to be purchased at a fixed price:* if you have already agreed a price with a supplier, you should include that figure.
- *Increase in money coming in*: remember that if inflation occurs, you may also increase your fees and charges. Include this in your budget for money coming in.

However you calculate the budget items, it is essential to keep a record of your working figures which can be shown to donors. This is especially important if you estimate the budget incorrectly. Donors may be willing to consider giving you a supplementary grant, but only if you can show how the original budget was calculated, and what has happened to change it.

Keeping to the budget

Preparing the budget is the first step. However, it is vital to compare the budget figures with what has actually happened as you go through the year. Advice on monitoring the budget is included in Chapter 9.

Key points of this chapter

- Establish your objectives, and involve everyone in the decisions.
- Decide what is needed to fulfil these objectives.
- Work out the costs, with help from other people.
- Write the costs down, item by item, for a fixed period of time.
- Record details of money coming in and money going out month by month.
- Use the budget and the cash-flow forecast when applying for funds.
- Prepare a similar budget for each year.
- When an increase in prices is likely to occur, include these costs in the budget, and keep a record of all your calculations.

Activities for Chapter 2 *solutions in Appendix C*

2.1 A group called *Training for Development* has recently started to provide courses.

Courses take place near to where the participants live. List the items of 'money coming in' and 'money going out' that may occur during the first year.

Money coming in   **Money going out**

2.2 Using the following information on what *Training for Development* is expecting next year, make a list of the main amounts (only) that you expect for each item of 'money coming in' and 'money going out'. Calculate the total for each section of the budget. (Note: extra information is included here for use with Activity 2.3.)

- The group has already been allocated a 'start-up' grant of 25,000.00 by the Department of Education to cover the cost of office and training equipment.

- Two grants from donors of 30,000.00 and 40,000.00 have been confirmed.

- Fees for training are expected to be 66,000.00 (based on 10 courses per month producing 550.00 each). The proceeds from the sale of materials are estimated at 1,200.00 (based on sales worth 100.00 per month).

- The group's Co-ordinator will be paid 12,000.00 per year; the Administrator will receive 9,000.00 per year; and four part-time trainers, will each be paid 6,000.00 per year. All these salaries include employer's taxes.

- The fixed contract for rent of an office has been agreed at 12,000.00 per year.
- There will be the following yearly costs:
  * electricity (7,000.00), water and telephone (10,000.00 combined), making a total of 17,000.00;
  * training materials 6,000.00 (based on 10 courses per month at 50.00 per course);
  * office expenses (including an audit fee of 5,000.00 and other costs at 750.00 per month), totalling 14,000.00;
  * travel and accommodation costs of 18,000.00 (based on five people at 300.00 per month);
  * hire of training rooms 21,000.00 (based on five courses per month at 350.00 each; other accommodation will be provided by trainees' own organization).
- Office equipment will cost 13,000.00 (four desks at 500.00; seven chairs at 250.00; filing cabinet at 700.00; additional furniture for offices at 8,550.00) and training equipment 11,000.00 (projector and screen at 4,800.00; television at 3,000.00; and audio equipment at 3,200.00).

Money coming in		**Money going out**	
Item	Amount	Item	Amount

2.3 Using the details in Activity 2.2, write notes to accompany the budget. These should provide the detailed calculations for the budget figures. (The first two notes have been included to start you off.)

Notes

1. Funding is confirmed for all grants.
2. Fees for training, based on 10 courses per month, producing 550.00 each.

2.4 If you were donating funds to *Training for Development*, what questions would you ask the group when you received a copy of the details you have listed in 2.2 and the notes in 2.3? What additional information might the group provide to accompany the budget, to anticipate these questions?

<u>Questions for</u>   <u>Information to provide</u>
Training for Development

2.5 Having prepared its budget, the group has provided details of when money will come in and go out (see below). Use this information to complete an outline cash-flow forecast (Figure 4) for April to December by:

a. Entering the amounts of 'money coming in' and totalling them.

b. Entering the amounts of 'money going out' and totalling them.

c. Calculating the closing balance at the end of each month.

The forecast for the first three months has been done for you.

Training for Development's list showing money coming in and going out

Budget item	Money coming in
• 'Start-up' grant (Dept of Education) 25,000	Received January
• Grants from donors 30,000	Received January/May (half each)
40,000	Received June
• Fees for training 66,000	Received monthly
• Sale of materials 1,200	Received monthly

	Money going out
• Co-ordinator's salary 12,000 per year	Paid monthly
• Administrator's salary 9,000 per year	Paid monthly
• Four part-time trainers' salaries at 6,000 each per year, totalling 24,000	Paid monthly
• Office rent 12,000 per year	Paid January/June (half each)
• Water charges 7,000 per year	Paid January
• Electricity and telephone, total 10,000 per year	Paid March/June/ September/December (quarterly)
• Training materials 6,000 per year	Paid monthly
• Office expenses 14,000 per year (including audit fee of 5,000)	Paid monthly (audit fee paid December)
• Travel and accommodation 18,000 per year	Paid monthly
• Hire of training room 21,000 per year	Paid monthly
• Purchases of office equipment 13,000 and training equipment 11,000	Paid January

Figure 4 *Training for Development cash-flow forecast for 1 January to 31 December*

	JAN	FEB	MAR	APR	MAY	JUN	JUL	AUG	SEP	OCT	NOV	DEC	TOTAL
Money coming in													
DOE 'start-up' grant	25,000												
Grant – donor 1	15,000												
Grant – donor 2													
Fees for training	5,500	5,500	5,500										
Sale of materials	100	100	100										
Total [A]	**45,600**	**5,600**	**5,600**										
Money going out													
Co-ordinator's salary	1,000	1,000	1,000										
Administrator's salary	750	750	750										
Trainers' salaries	2,000	2,000	2,000										
Office rent	6,000												
Electricity, water, telephone	7,000		2,500										
Training materials	500	500	500										
Office expenses (incl. audit)	750	750	750										
Travel/accommodation	1,500	1,500	1,500										
Hire of training rooms	1,750	1,750	1,750										
Office equipment	13,000												
Training equipment	11,000												
Total [B]	**45,250**	**8,250**	**10,750**										
Money at start of month [C]	0	350	(2,300)	(7,450)									
Plus total money coming in [A]	45,600	5,600	5,600										
Less total money going out [B]	45,250	8,250	10,750										
Money at end of month [C+A–B]	**350**	**(2,300)**	**(7,450)**										

Brackets around the figure show wit is a negative amount.
The monthly totals of money coming in and going out are identified by the letters [A] and [B] respectively. Letter [C] is the amount at the beginning of each month. The amount held at the end of each month becomes the money at the start of the following month.

2.6   On the evidence of the cash-flow forecast, what problems
       are likely to arise for *Training for Development*? How could
       these problems be solved?

       Problems   **Solutions**

2.7   If a donor saw this cash-flow forecast, what comments
       would you expect to receive?

       Comments from the donor

2.8   If you have access to a computer, try putting the solution
       to Activity 2.5 on to a spreadsheet program.

CHAPTER 3

Records of money coming in and going out

This chapter shows how to record money coming in and going out of a group or organization, and how to make sure there is a piece of paper to back up every transaction. It shows how to keep a cash book record, and how to complete and file income and payment receipts that are cross-referenced to the cash book. The chapter outlines some of the basic controls when dealing with cash, for example the need to count the cash regularly and agree the amount with your accounting records. There are activities to complete which will build your confidence in completing your records.

Keywords: record of money received and paid; cash book; rules to control cash; example of receipt; cash count

One of the most important rules in keeping accounts *is to make sure that everything is written down, and that every piece of paper is kept.* However, without any previous experience of keeping accounts it is difficult to know how to write things down. This chapter will show you the way to do it.

Recording the money

Firstly, you can divide the finances of your group into two parts: money coming in, and money going out. You will need a book to use for this purpose only. It is called a **cash book**, because it records money (cash) coming in and going out. You

http://dx.doi.org/10.3362/9781780448206.003

can either buy a cash book with lines already drawn, or use an exercise book and draw your own lines.

This page is then ready for you to write down any money that comes in or goes out of the group, the date when it happens, what it is, how much it is, and (in the balance column) how much cash is left.

Figure 5 Layout of a simple cash book

CASH BOOK				
Date	Details	Cash amount IN	Cash amount OUT	Balance

Figure 6 gives an example of a completed cash book. This example, and others that follow, assume that the group had some cash available to use at the beginning of the month. This is referred to as the **opening balance**.

Figure 6 shows a record of cash coming in and going out. It also gives the balance of cash after each entry has been included. This is important, because it shows how much should remain, and lets you count the actual cash to make sure it agrees with the cash book. The cash must be counted regularly. If the amount you have counted does not agree with the balance in the cash book, it may be that you have miscounted the cash, forgotten to write something down, or made an error in addition or subtraction (mistakes which you can correct). More seriously, it could be that some money has been lost or stolen. If so, it is essential to know this as soon as possible and alert the group leader.

Figure 6 Example of a completed cash book

CASH BOOK				
Date	Details	Cash amount IN	Cash amount OUT	Balance
1 Jan	Opening balance	1,000.00		1,000.00
3 Jan	Grant from donor	9,500.00		10,500.00
3 Jan	Stationery for office		10.00	10,490.00
5 Jan	Purchase of medical supplies		650.00	9,840.00
7 Jan	Driver's salary		200.00	9,640.00
7 Jan	Purchase of drugs		3,450.00	6,190.00
9 Jan	Grant from Dept of Health	7,000.00		13,190.00
9 Jan	Sale of drugs	14.50		13,204.50
10 Jan	Cash to bank (grant paid in)		7,000.00	6,204.50

Figure 6 shows that 7,000.00 cash was paid into the bank on 10 January. This was the grant, received on 9 January. (Chapter 5 shows how this would be accounted for in the bank records.)

As far as possible the recording of entries should be in date order. We said earlier that it is important to write everything down, and that every piece of paper relating to money should be kept. We will now look at the pieces of paper that you are likely to need.

Payment receipts

When you pay an amount in cash, for example the driver's salary in Figure 6, you could just hand over the money. However, one day, the driver might claim that he or she was not paid. Although you may be certain that you did pay the salary, there would be no written proof of this.

To avoid this situation arising, every time you pay a salary, or indeed any other item, you must ask the person receiving the money to sign, or make their mark/thumb-print, for it. This signed piece of paper is called a **receipt**. All receipts must

Figure 7 Example of a receipt

GROUP NAME	
	Receipt number ....
Date	Amount ....
Received from	
Description	
Received by	

be kept together in a separate file. Figure 7 shows an example of a receipt. Some people refer to receipts as **vouchers**.

Each receipt should be numbered (if possible, they should all be pre-numbered before you start to use them), and its number should be written against the entry in the cash book, as shown in Figure 8. This makes it easier to find the receipt.

If any other paperwork is available (such as a request for payment from a merchant or supplier – called an **invoice**), this too should be attached to the receipt and filed. In the future, these documents will show exactly what happened.

Income receipts

In the same way, when people give money to your group, they will want a receipt from you, to prove that they have paid you the money. Even if they do not ask for one, it is good practice to give them a receipt. You will need to keep a duplicate copy of this for your own records, which should be filed in an income receipts file.

The format of an income receipt can be the same as the payment receipt, but it is helpful to distinguish them in some way – perhaps by a different colour – and to have a different sequence of receipt numbers, as shown in Figure 8 (500 to 502). Again, the receipts should be pre-numbered and these numbers should be included in the cash book for reference.

Figure 8 Example of a cash book with receipt numbers

CASH BOOK					
Date	Details	Receipt number	Cash amount IN Receipts	Cash amount OUT Payments	Balance
1 Jan	Opening balance		1,000.00		1,000.00
3 Jan	Grant from donor	500	9,500.00		10,500.00
3 Jan	Stationery for office	1		10.00	10,490.00
5 Jan	Purchase of medical supplies	2		650.00	9,840.00
7 Jan	Driver's salary	3		200.00	9,640.00
7 Jan	Purchase of drugs	4		3,450.00	6,190.00
9 Jan	Grant from Dept of Health	501	7,000.00		13,190.00
9 Jan	Sale of drugs	502	14.50		13,204.50
10 Jan	Cash to bank	–		7,000.00	6,204.50

Unfortunately, the word 'receipts' has two meanings. Firstly, it means these signed pieces of paper. But secondly, accountants and book-keepers use it to mean *money coming in*. It has a similar meaning to the word 'income'. When the word 'receipts' is used for money coming in, the word used for money going out is 'payments'.

For the remainder of this book, we will use the words 'receipts' and 'payments' to describe money coming in and going out. The cash book will then look like the example in Figure 8. (Note that the opening balance is the cash already held, so it does not need a receipt number.)

Another method of presentation

Receipts and payments may be shown on separate pages of the cash book, which would look like the example in Figure 9.

This needs more space in your book, and no 'balance' column is shown. To find the balance (at any time), you need

to add up all the payment amounts, and subtract this total
from the total of the opening balance plus all the receipts
amounts. You can then total the cash columns (as shown in
Figure 9), and write down the closing balance. (Note there are
no cash entries in this example after 10 January.)

Whichever way the cash book is presented, a total of the
cash balance must be shown at the end of each month. You
will also wish to calculate a cash balance during the month,
possibly daily or weekly. This will make sure that the balance
is the same as the cash that is actually held.

At the beginning of each month, start a new page in your
cash book, and write in the opening balance figure, which is
the **closing balance** at the end of the previous month.

Figure 9 Example of a cash book with receipts and payments shown separately

RECEIPTS				PAYMENTS			
Date	Details	Receipt number	Cash amount	Date	Details	Payment number	Cash amount
1 Jan	Opening balance		1,000.00	3 Jan	Stationery for office	1	10.00
3 Jan	Grant from donor	500	9,500.00	5 Jan	Purchase of medical supplies	2	650.00
9 Jan	Grant from Dept. of Health	501	7,000.00	7 Jan	Driver's salary	3	200.00
9 Jan	Sale of drugs	502	14.50	7 Jan	Purchase of drugs	4	3,450.00
				10 Jan	Cash to bank	–	7,000.00
	Total		**17,514.50**		**Total**		**11,310.00**

Closing balance (10 January)   6,204.50

Rules to help you to control your cash

So far, we have looked at accounting for money, but not at the
actual cash itself (that is, the notes and coins). There are a few
rules to make your cash control much easier:

1. Always keep your cash secure, preferably in a lockable tin, which is kept in a safe or locked cupboard. Keep the key securely.
2. Make sure that only one person is responsible for the cash. Whenever a new person takes on this task, the outgoing person and the incoming person should count the cash and agree the amount together. This should be written down and signed by both.
3. Ideally, the person responsible for the cash should be a different person from the one keeping the accounts.
4. Someone in a senior position within the group (for example, the group leader) should count the cash regularly, and agree the figure with the cash book. This helps the person looking after the cash, because it shows him or her to be honest.
5. A senior person should also authorize any large or unusual payments. You may like to set a limit, beyond which the person handling the money should obtain (written) approval for expenditure.
6. Always issue receipts for any cash received or paid, and make an entry in the cash book.
7. It is often possible to obtain insurance to cover the holding of cash. If amounts are large, it is worth considering this. (If you do, remember to include the cost of this in your budget.)
8. You should know in advance how much cash you are likely to need. Don't wait until you need to pay someone before realizing that you have no money left.
9. If your group's money is running out, take action as soon as possible.

Key points of this chapter

- Keep all documents relating to the accounts.
- There should be a piece of paper to support every transaction.
- Open a cash book to record money coming in (receipts) and money going out (payments).

- Record all details as you go along, in date order.
- Remember that the word 'receipts' has two meanings: one relates to money received, the other relates to the piece of paper which says that an amount of money has changed hands.
- Have pre-numbered receipts available to be signed by people to whom you give money, and for you to sign when you are given money.
- File paper receipts (vouchers) for receipts and for payments separately, along with any other relevant paperwork.
- Include the receipt numbers in your cash book as a reference.
- Count the cash regularly, and agree the total with the balance in your cash book.
- Make sure that you use the rules to control your cash.

The cash book will be enough to record what is happening to the cash for very small groups. The next chapter will however show you a way of arranging the information in a more useful order for groups which have more than, say, 20 or 30 entries in the cash book each month.

Activities for Chapter 3 *solutions in Appendix C*

3.1   *Training for Development* began its work in January. The
following details show what the group received and paid
out.

Money coming in		Amount
January 1	Fees for training	1,300
January 4	Fees for training	2,800
January 10	Sale of booklet	25
January 15	Fees for training	1,350
January 20	Sale of materials	15
January 27	Sale of booklet	25

Money going out		
January 4	Purchase of stationery	400
January 4	Purchase of desks	1,000
January 7	Photocopying training booklets	200
January 7	Purchase of training materials	900
January 9	Purchase of stationery	250
January 10	Hire of training rooms	400
January 14	Purchase of filing cabinet	700
January 19	Travel expenses: Co-ordinator	320
January 25	Purchase of small office items	240

a. Enter the above information in to the cash book in
Figure 10. Enter the items from the *money coming
in* and *money going out* sections in date order. A few
entries have been included to start you off.

b. Calculate the balance after each transaction.

Figure 10 *Training for Development* cash book

Date	Details	Cash amount IN	Cash amount OUT	Balance
1 Jan	Opening balance			0
1 Jan	Fees for training	1,300		1,300
4 Jan	Fees for training	2,800		4,100
4 Jan	Purchase of stationery		400	3,700

3.2   Using Figures 11a to 11f, write a receipt for each of the items in the 'money coming in' section. The first two have already been completed. When you have completed these, add the title 'receipt number' to the spare column of your cash book in Figure 10 and include the appropriate numbers.

Figure 11a

TRAINING FOR DEVELOPMENT	
	Receipt number **1**
Date *1 January*	Amount *1,300.00*
Received from	*(name of person giving cash)*
Description	*Fees for training*
Received by	*A Cashier*

Figure 11b

TRAINING FOR DEVELOPMENT	
	Receipt number **2**
Date *4 January*	Amount *2,800.00*
Received from	*(name of person giving cash)*
Description	*Fees for training*
Received by	*A Cashier*

Figure 11c

TRAINING FOR DEVELOPMENT	
	Receipt number **3**
Date	Amount ....
Received from	
Description	
Received by	

Figure 11d

TRAINING FOR DEVELOPMENT
Receipt number **4**
Date .... Amount ....
Received from ....
Description ....
Received by ....

Figure 11e

TRAINING FOR DEVELOPMENT
Receipt number **5**
Date .... Amount ....
Received from ....
Description ....
Received by ....

Figure 11f

TRAINING FOR DEVELOPMENT
Receipt number **6**
Date .... Amount ....
Received from ....
Description ....
Received by ....

Figure 12 *Training for Development* cash book ('receipts' and payments' shown separately)

	RECEIPTS				PAYMENTS			
Date	Details	Receipt number	Cash amount	Date	Details	Payment number	Cash amount
1 Jan	Opening balance		0				
	Total				Total		

Closing balance (31 January)

3.3 a. Using Figure 12 (previous page), use the same information given in Activity 3.1 to prepare the cash book showing 'receipts' and 'payments'.

b. Enter the 'receipt numbers' from Activity 3.2; and the 'payment number' for payments in a sequence starting with P1.

c. Total the two cash amount columns.

d. Calculate the closing balance at 31 January (total receipts *less* total payments) and enter this figure below the table. (Check to see that it is the same figure shown in Activity 3.1.)

3.4 After the cash book has been prepared, the actual cash in the cash box will be counted. Figure 13 shows the notes and coins that are in *Training for Development's* cash box.

Figure 13 *Training for Development* cash counted in cash box at 31 January

Value of notes	Number of notes
20	11
50	8
100	1
Value of coins	**Number of coins**
1	33
5	17
10	27

a. Use the table in Figure 14 to calculate the total amount of cash. Compare this with the balance as at 31 January shown in the cash book in Activity 3.3.

b. Explain the action you would take if there were any difference.

Figure 14 *Training for Development* cash count as at 31 January

Cash counted:

	Value	multiplied by	Number	equals	Total value
Notes:	20	×		=	
	50	×		=	
	100	×		=	
Coins:	1	×		=	
	5	×		=	
	10	×		=	

Total cash counted

Cash book balance at 31 January

Difference* (if any)

*Action taken regarding any difference:

Counted by .... Date .... Agreed by .... Date ....

3.5 Which of the answers a–d do you consider the most appropriate for each of the following questions? State the reason why you have chosen this answer.

1. Where, ideally, should cash be kept at night?

a. Anywhere, as long as it is in a locked tin.

b. In a locked tin placed in a lockable cupboard or safe.

c. Taken home by the person responsible.

d. Left with the office guard until the person responsible returns the next day.

Reason ....

2. What should the person responsible for the cash do if the group is running out of money?

a. Alert the group leader as soon as possible.

b. Keep going until all the money is used up.

c. Ensure there is enough money to pay for essential items.

d. Ask friends to provide a loan.

Reason ....

3. If payment for a large unusual item is required, what should the cashier do?

a. Pay it if there is enough money available.

b. See if the item is in the budget before payment is made.

c. Obtain written approval from a senior person within the group.

d. Go to the bank to obtain more money.

Reason ....

4. Why should a receipt be issued each time cash is received?

a. So that the person paying the money has proof of payment.

b. In case an auditor inspects the accounts.

c. To make sure proper control of cash is in place.

d. In case the cash book is lost.

Reason ....

CHAPTER 4

Arranging your records to give more information

One of the limitations of the cash book is that although it tells you exactly what cash has come in and gone out and the balance of cash left, it does not tell you anything about what part of the budget the money was used for. This chapter shows a technique for providing this information by adding extra columns to the cash book. It is known as an 'analysed cash book'. It has some of the benefits of more complex accounting systems, without the need for technical accounting knowledge. The activities build on the examples in previous chapters to show how an analysed cash book can be used and maintained.

Keywords: cash book; analysed cash book; budget headings; cash book columns; book-keeping

If you have read Chapter 3, and you think that the way of completing a cash book shown there is sufficient for your group, there is no need to read this chapter. However, if you want to extract more information from your accounts, or if you just want to make sure you are not missing anything, then read on!

One of the problems with the cash book which we looked at in Chapter 3 is that, although it will tell you exactly what cash has come in and gone out, and the balance of cash left, it does not tell you anything about the money.

http://dx.doi.org/10.3362/9781780448206.004

The analysed cash book

You are likely to need to know, for example, how much of the money recorded in the cash book refers to income from grants, rather than income from sales, and how much has been spent on salaries, rather than on purchase of medicines. With only a few entries in the cash book, you can easily add them up. However, as the number of entries increases, you need to have a system to help. This is done in an **analysed cash book**, which, in addition to the cash book columns, has extra columns which show what *type* of money it is. More space will be required when completing an analysed cash book, so you need either to rule up a larger book, or to buy a book ready ruled.

Let us look at an example, using the same figures as we used in the previous chapter. Because of lack of space to show the receipts and payments parts of the cash book side by side, we will first look at the receipts side (Figure 15), and then at the payments side (Figure 16).

A few points to note from the analysed cash book:

- The figure received or paid is always listed in the amount column and then again in one of the other columns.
- The headings are the same as those included in the budget. This will help when you compare the actual figures with the budget figures.
- There is an extra column, called 'other', on both the receipts side and the payments side. This is useful in practice, because items arise which do not belong under any one heading. If a payment, for example, does appear in this column, you may well want to question why it was spent, because it would not have been included in the budget.
- On the payments side on 10 January the 'cash to bank' item represents money paid into the bank. In these cash records it is shown in the 'other' column. Chapter 5 will show how this item is recorded in the bank records.

Figure 15 Receipts side of an analysed cash book

Date	Details	Receipt number	Cash amount	Opening balance	Grants	Sale of drugs	Other receipts
1 Jan	Opening balance		1,000.00	1,000.00			
3 Jan	Grant from donor	500	9,500.00		9,500.00		
9 Jan	Grant from Dept of Health	501	7,000.00		7,000.00		
9 Jan	Sale of drugs	502	14.50			14.50	
31 Jan	Totals		17,514.50	1,000.00	16,500.00	14.50	–

Figure 16 Payments side of an analysed cash book

Date	Details	Payment number	Cash amount	Salaries	Rent	Drugs	Medical supplies	Electricity	Office expenses	Other payments
3 Jan	Stationery for office	1	10.00						10.00	
5 Jan	Purchase of medical supplies	2	650.00				650.00			
7 Jan	Driver's salary	3	200.00	200.00						
7 Jan	Purchase of drugs	4	3,450.00			3,450.00				
10 Jan	Cash to bank	–	7,000.00							7,000.00
31 Jan	Totals		11,310.00	200.00	–	3,450.00	650.00	–	10.00	7,000.00

- At the end of the month, you need to add up all the columns. The total of all the analysed receipts columns (ignoring the amount column) should add up to the total of the receipts amount column. (In Figure 15, for example, 1,000.00 + 16,500.00 + 14.50 = 17,514.50.) If not, you have entered something in the wrong place. (Remember you have entered each item in two columns.)
- Similarly, the total of all the analysed payments columns (other than the amount column) should add up to the total of the payments amount column. (In Figure 16, for example, 200.00 + 3,450.00 + 650.00 + 10.00 + 7,000.00 = 11,310.00.)
- The cash balance can be obtained by subtracting the total of the payments amount column from the total of the receipts amount column.

Key points of this chapter

- An analysed cash book will be useful if you have more than 20 or 30 entries in your cash book each month. It will give you more details of the money you have received and paid.
- You will need more space for this, and it is easier if the receipts and payments are on separate pages.
- Each part will have an amount column, and analysis columns drawn up using the headings from the budget.
- The amount received or paid is always entered twice: once in the amount column, and once in an analysis column.

The total of the receipts amount column will be equal to the total of all the receipts analysis columns. This will also be the case for payments.

Activities for Chapter 4 *solutions in Appendix C*

4.1 Complete the following sentences:
- The extra columns of an analysed cash book show the .... of money that has been spent.

- The headings of the columns in an analysed cash book should follow those shown in the .... Some categories might have to be grouped together because there is a limited number of ....

- It is good practice to have a column entitled .... on each of the receipts and payments sides of an analysed cash book.

- At the end of the month the columns should be .... The total of all totals of the analysed columns for receipts should be the same as the total amount of the .... column.

- The cash balance at the end of the month can be found by subtracting the total amount of the column for .... from the total amount of the column for ....

4.2 *Training for Development* wishes to provide further information in its cash book. It will use the budget headings in the receipts and payments columns. They are as follows:

Receipts
- Grants from donors
- Fees for training
- Sale of materials
- Other receipts

Payments

- Salaries
- Rent/electricity/water/telephone charges
- Training materials
- Office expenses (including audit fee)
- Travel/accommodation
- Hire of training rooms
- Office/training equipment
- Other payments

a. Using Figures 17a and 17b, and the information shown in the cash book (from Activity 3.1), prepare an analysed cash book for the month of January.

b. When the information has been included, add up the columns and make sure that the total of the analysis columns is the same as the total of the cash amount column.

4.3 If you have access to a computer, try preparing the analysed cash book in Activity 4.2 on a spreadsheet program.

Figure 17a *Training for development* analysed cash book (receipts side)

Date	Details	Receipt number	Cash amount	Opening balance	Grants from donors	Fees for training	Sale of materials	Other receipts
1 Jan	Opening balance		0	0				
	Totals							

Figure 17b *Training for Development* analysed cash book (payments side)

Date	Details	Payment number	Cash amount	Salaries	Rent/ electricity/ water/ telephone	Training materials	Office expenses (incl. audit)	Travel/ accommo- dation	Hire of training rooms	Office/ training equipment	Other payments
Totals											

Closing balance

CHAPTER 5

Bank accounts

Here we consider the types of account that banks will offer, how to complete the appropriate records, and how to account for money paid into the bank from cash, or for cheques cashed at the bank. The chapter identifies some important points to remember when completing these records and also shows alternative presentations for groups and organizations. A number of activities are included to give practice in completing the records.

Keywords: bank accounts; bank book; accounting for transfers between bank and cash; types of bank account offered; cash and bank book

As any group grows, there comes a point when it can no longer rely on cash for everything. It will also need to use a bank account.

What the bank will offer

Most banks can operate a range of accounts for you.

Current account

A **current account** is the most common type of account. It is sometimes referred to as a **cheque** (or **check**) **account**. You can pay money in, and write cheques to make payments, as often as you like (as long as there is enough money in the

http://dx.doi.org/10.3362/9781780448206.005

account!). Sometimes it is possible to take more money out
than you have in the account; this is called an **overdraft**. It
can only be done with the agreement of the bank, and you will
have to pay to do it; the charge is called **interest**.

Banks will often make a charge for operating your account
(called a **bank charge**). They are unlikely to pay you interest
on a current account.

Deposit and savings accounts

If you have money which you do not need for some time, it
can often be placed in a **deposit account**. The bank is likely
to pay you **interest** for holding the money in the deposit
account, but you will usually have to tell the bank in advance
if you want the money repaid. Your bank may also offer you
a **savings account**, paying a different rate of interest from a
deposit account, possibly with extra restrictions, for example
giving a month's advance notice to take money out of the
account. Sometimes the deposit and savings accounts are the
same.

How to account for bank accounts

Accounting for your money at the bank is similar to accounting
for cash. Instead of a cash book you need a **bank book**. This
is *your* record of your money at the bank, and it should be
kept accurately. Sometimes the term cash book is used (rather
than bank book) to mean the cash *and* bank records. Here we
will distinguish between the two records by using the separate
names.

You can buy a bank book, or draw lines in an exercise book,
as with the cash book. In reality, it may be the same physical
book, with the cash part at the beginning and maybe the bank
part towards the end. It is also useful to have separate pages
(usually opposite each other) in the bank book for money
coming into the account and money going out of it. Figure 18
shows an example.

Figure 18 Example of entries in a bank book

RECEIPTS				PAYMENTS				
Date	Details	Paying-in reference	Bank amount	Date	Details	Payment number	Cheque number	Bank amount
1 Jan	Opening balance		0	10 Jan	Rent of premises	5	1701	2,500.00
10 Jan	Cash to bank (grant paid in)	856	7,000.00	11 Jan	Medical supplies	6	1702	3,000.00
10 Jan	Sale of drugs	857	20.00	16 Jan	Purchase of drugs	7	1703	550.00
12 Jan	Sale of medical supplies	858	127.00	27 Jan	Office equipment	8	1704	100.00
	Total		7,147.00		Total			6,150.00
					Closing balance (31 January)			997.00

In the bank book people often use the 'paying-in reference' as a receipt number. Therefore the 'receipt number' column is not needed because any paperwork will be filed under the paying-in reference number. Items received into the bank account will not need a receipt in the way that cash receipts do.

As with the cash book, we can obtain an up-to-date or closing bank book balance by subtracting the payments total from the receipts total. In this case the balance will be 7,147.00 *less* 6,150.00 = 997.00.

If you have more than one bank account (for example, a current account and a deposit account), it is important to keep a separate bank book, or separate pages in the same bank book, for each account.

Transfers between cash and bank

When cash is paid into the bank account, or when a cheque is written for cash, this will affect both your cash book and bank book. Firstly, if you pay cash into the bank (as on 10 January), your cash balance will *decrease*, and your bank balance will *increase*. Your cash and bank books will look like Figure 19.

Secondly, if you decide that your cash is low and you wish to withdraw money from your bank account by writing a cheque, your bank balance will *decrease*, and your cash balance will *increase*. Your cash and bank books will then look like Figure 20.

Always remember to make entries in both your cash book and your bank book, if you pay cash into or take cash out of the bank.

Figure 19 Entries in your records when cash is paid into the bank

BANK BOOK RECEIPTS			
Date	Details	Paying-in reference	Bank amount
10 Jan	Cash to bank	856	7,000.00

CASH BOOK PAYMENTS			
Date	Details	Payment number	Cash amount
10 Jan	Cash to bank		7,000.00

Your cash balance will *decrease* and your bank balance will *increase*.

Figure 20 Entries in your records when cash is taken out of the bank

CASH BOOK RECEIPTS			
Date	Details	Receipt number	Cash amount
14 Feb	Bank to cash		600.00

BANK BOOK PAYMENTS			
Date	Details	Payment number	Cheque number	Bank amount
14 Feb	Bank to cash		1708	600.00

Your bank balance will *decrease* and your cash balance will *increase*.

Points to remember when filling in your bank book

1. The bank may give you a **bank paying-in book** with which to pay cash and cheques into your account. Each form has either two copies, one for the bank and a copy for you to keep, or one form plus a 'stub' for you to retain. If the bank does not give you a special book, it will provide paying-in slips for this purpose, and you should retain a copy of the slip, which the bank should stamp and initial. This is proof that you have paid the money in. The bank paying-in slip (if available) should then be filed according to the paying-in reference order (shown in Figures 18 and 19). If the number is not given by the bank you should start your own sequence.
2. The items received in your bank book will be either money that you have paid into the bank, or amounts that have been paid directly into your account by someone else. The bank will sometimes give you additional details about money paid in by other people. You should file this information from the bank together with the paying-in slips.
3. The payments part of your bank book includes a column for a payment number. You could ask the person receiving a cheque to sign a receipt (as you should in the case of cash), but it is not so important to obtain a receipt for cheque payments. Many organizations do not bother with receipts for payment by cheque. However, it is useful to start a sequence of 'payment number' references, whether or not receipts are received. All paperwork (for example invoices) can then be filed in order of the payment numbers.
4. Each time a payment is made, the cheque number (or its last three or four digits) should be recorded in the bank book.

Two other methods of presentation

It is possible to arrange the bank book in an analysed format, as shown with the cash book in Chapter 4. Extra columns would be needed to record the paying-in references and cheque numbers. Another possible presentation would be to combine the cash and bank book columns into one book. The column headings would then look like Figure 21. This method looks slightly more complicated than keeping separate books, but it means that all related information is kept in one place. Find the presentation which suits your group best. As mentioned above, this combined book can be called simply the 'cash book', even though it contains bank entries as well.

Key points of this chapter

- There are different types of bank accounts: current, deposit, and savings.
- Start a bank book and enter in it everything that happens in the bank account.
- Use a separate page in the bank book for items coming in (receipts) and items going out (payments).
- An analysed bank book will show you the type of payment made from the bank.
- You can combine the cash book and the bank book. Sometimes this combined book is simply called the 'cash book'.
- When transfers of money are made between bank and cash, always remember to make an entry in both records.

Figure 21 Headings of a combined cash and bank book

RECEIPTS					PAYMENTS					
Date	Details	Receipt number	Paying-in reference	Cash amount	Bank amount	Date	Details	Payment number	Cheque number	Cash amount	Bank amount

Activities for Chapter 5 *solutions in Appendix C*

5.1 List all that you know about these three topics:

- bank current account;
- bank deposit account;
- the difference between cash and bank amounts, in accounting.

5.2 The following amounts were paid through *Training for Development's* bank account in January. (Paying-in references or cheque numbers are shown in the reference column.)

		Amount	Reference
Money paid directly into the bank			
5 January	'Start-up' grant	25,000	201
14 January	Grant from donor 1	15,000	202
15 January	Fees for training	480	203
Money paid out by cheque			
4 January	Rent	6,000	406781
7 January	Purchase of office chairs	1,750	406782
16 January	Water charge	6,670	406783
16 January	Purchase of projector and screen	4,800	406784
18 January	Hire of training room	890	406786
24 January	Purchase of television	3,000	406787
24 January	Accommodation: Co-ordinator	400	406788
31 January	Salaries	3,225	406789

a. Using Figure 22, prepare the bank book, showing 'receipts' and 'payments'.

b. Enter the 'paying-in references', 'payment numbers', and 'cheque numbers'. Start the 'payment numbers' with a new sequence starting with P701.

c. Total the two bank amount columns.

d. Calculate the closing bank balance at 31 January and enter this below the table.

Figure 22 *Training for Development* bank book

RECEIPTS					PAYMENTS				
Date	Details	Paying-in reference	Bank amount		Date	Details	Payment number	Cheque number	Bank amount
1 Jan	Opening balance		0						
	Total					Total			

Closing balance (31 January) _____

5.3 Using Figure 23, prepare a combined cash and bank book, based on the information contained in activities 3.1 and 5.2. Some of the information has already been included.

Notes about the completion

- The entries are in date order, regardless of whether they are cash or bank.

- The 'payment numbers' could be in one sequence for both cash and bank payments. This example, however, has retained the two sequences of numbers used in previous activities.

Figure 23 *Training for Development* cash and bank record (combined cash and bank record)

RECEIPTS						PAYMENTS					
Date	Details	Receipt number	Paying-in reference	Cash amount	Bank amount	Date	Details	Payment number	Cheque number	Cash amount	Bank amount
1 Jan	Opening balance					4 Jan	Rent	P701	406781		
1 Jan	Fees for training	1				4 Jan	Purchase of stationery	P1			
4 Jan	Fees for training	2				4 Jan	Purchase of desks	P2			
5 Jan	'Start-up' grant		201			7 Jan	Photocopying	P3			
10 Jan	Sale of booklet	3				7 Jan	Purchase of office chairs	P702	406782		
14 Jan	Grant		202			7 Jan	Purchase of training materials	P4			
15 Jan	Fees for training		203			9 Jan	Purchase of stationery	P5			
15 Jan	Fees for training	4				10 Jan	Hire of training rooms	P6			
20 Jan	Sale of materials	5				14 Jan	Purchase of filing cabinet	P7			
27 Jan	Sale of booklet	6				16 Jan	Water charge	P703	406783		
						16 Jan	Purchase of projector and screen	P704	406784		
						18 Jan	Hire of training rooms	P705	406786		
						19 Jan	Travel: Co-ordinator	P8			
						24 Jan	Purchase of television	P706	406787		
						24 Jan	Accommodation: Co-ordinator	P707	406788		
						25 Jan	Purchase of small office items	P9			
						31 Jan	Salaries	P708	406789		
	Total						Total				

Closing balance (31 January)

5.4 Using Figures 24a and 24b, prepare an analysed cash and bank book, based on the information contained in activities 3.1 and 5.2. Some of the information has already been included.

Figure 24a *Training for Development* analysed cash and bank book (receipts side)

Date	Details	Receipt number	Paying-in reference	Cash amount	Bank amount	Opening balance	Grants from donors	Fees for training	Sale of materials	Other receipts
1 Jan	Opening balance			0	0	0				
1 Jan	Fees for training	1								
4 Jan	Fees for training	2								
5 Jan	'Start-up' grant		201							
10 Jan	Sale of booklet	3								
14 Jan	Grant		202							
15 Jan	Fees for training		203							
15 Jan	Fees for training	4								
20 Jan	Sale of materials	5								
27 Jan	Sale of booklet	6								
	Total									

Figure 24b *Training for Development* analysed cash and bank book (payments side)

Date	Details	Payment number	Cheque number	Cash amount	Bank amount	Salaries	Rent/ electricity/ water/ telephone	Training materials	Office expenses (including audit)	Travel/ accommo-dation	Hire of training rooms	Office/ training equipment	Other payments
4 Jan	Rent	P701	406781										
4 Jan	Purchase of stationery	P1											
4 Jan	Purchase of desks	P2											
7 Jan	Photocopying	P3											
7 Jan	Purchase of office chairs	P702	406782										
7 Jan	Purchase of training materials	P4											
9 Jan	Purchase of stationery	P5											
10 Jan	Hire of training rooms	P6											
14 Jan	Purchase of filing cabinet	P7											
16 Jan	Water charge	P703	406783										
16 Jan	Purchase of projector and screen	P704	406784										
18 Jan	Hire of training rooms	P705	406786										
19 Jan	Travel: Co-ordinator	P8											
24 Jan	Purchase of television	P706	406787										
24 Jan	Accommodation: Co-ordinator	P707	406788										
25 Jan	Purchase of small office items	P9											
31 Jan	Salaries	P708	406789										
	Total												

Closing balance (31 January)

Transfers between bank and cash

5.5 In February, *Training for Development* had the following transactions:

10 February	Cash paid into the bank (paying-in reference 210)	1,200
12 February	Cheque written (cheque number 406795)	4,000

Record these transactions in the cash and bank book in Figure 25.

Figure 25 *Training for Development* cash and bank book

RECEIPTS					PAYMENTS						
Date	Details	Receipt number	Paying-in reference	Cash amount	Bank amount	Date	Details	Payment number	Cheque number	Cash amount	Bank amount

CHAPTER 6

Making sure your figures agree with the bank's figures

An important control for community organizations and small groups is to make sure that the internal records agree with how the bank has recorded your transactions. This chapter explains how this is done using a 'bank reconciliation statement' to compare your bank book to your bank statement (or bank pass book). The chapter takes you through the steps to agree or 'reconcile' the records, and illustrates this with examples. There are also activities to practise this technique and to build up confidence in using it. A number of rules are also given to help protect your bank account and its transactions against misuse.

Keywords: bank statement; bank reconciliation statement; accounting for bank transactions; rules to control your bank account

The bank will let you know how much money they think you have in your account. This will be shown in either a **bank statement** or a **bank pass book**. Bank statements tend to be more widely used, especially for current accounts.

Agreeing your records

Whenever you receive a bank statement, or have your bank book brought up to date, you must make sure that your bank book figures agree with the bank's and that you know the

http://dx.doi.org/10.3362/9781780448206.006

Figure 26 Outline of a bank reconciliation statement

BANK RECONCILIATION STATEMENT AS AT		
	Amount	**Total amount**
Bank balance at .... (from statement/pass book)	....	[A]
Less: cheques not yet included in the bank's records		
cheque number	....	
cheque number	....	.... [B: total cheques]
	Sub-total	[A–B]
Plus: items paid in but not yet included in the bank's records		
paying-in reference	....	[C]
Balance in bank book at .... (group's own record)	....	[A–B+C]

[The letters A, B, and C are included to show where calculations are made.]

reasons for any differences. This agreement of the two records is called a **reconciliation** or **bank reconciliation.** An outline of a table used is shown in Figure 26.

The example shown in Figure 27 shows the information you are likely to have available to reconcile. You will need to go through a number of stages to make sure that your bank book and the bank statement (pass book) reconcile:

1. Enter any outstanding items in your bank book to bring it up to date.
2. Include any charges or interest from the bank statement in your bank book.
3. Tick off the items that appear in your bank book *and* in the bank's records.
4. Construct a table (as shown in Figure 26) to show how the two records agree. Include all items that are not ticked off.

If your figures do not agree, check them again. If they still do not agree, it is worth checking the adding up on your statement/pass book: banks do sometimes make mistakes! Look through the example in Figures 27a, 27b and 28. Figure 27a shows examples of a bank book and bank statement. Figure 27b shows the same information, with the bank book updated and items in both this record and the bank statement ticked off. Figure 28 shows the bank reconciliation statement.

Figure 27a Example of a bank book and bank statement

BANK BOOK

	Receipts			Payments				
Date	Details	Paying-in reference	Bank amount	Date	Details	Payment number	Cheque number	Bank amount
1 Jan	Opening balance		0	10 Jan	Rent of premises	5	1701	2,500
10 Jan	Cash to bank (grant paid in)	856	7,000	11 Jan	Medical supplies	6	1702	3,000
10 Jan	Sale of drugs	857	20	16 Jan	Purchase of drugs	7	1703	550
12 Jan	Sale of medical supplies	858	127	27 Jan	Office equipment	8	1704	100
	Total		7,147		Total			6,150

Closing balance (7,147 *less* 6,150 =)   997

BANK STATEMENT

Date	Details	In	Out	Balance
1 Jan	Opening balance			0
10 Jan	Sundries 856	7,000		7,000
10 Jan	Sundries 857	20		7,020
14 Jan	Cheque 1702		3,000	4,020
19 Jan	Cheque 1703		550	3,470
31 Jan	Bank charges		20	3,450
31 Jan	Closing balance			3,450

Figure 27b Example of a bank book and bank statement, including updating of the bank book, and items in this record and the bank statement 'ticked off'

BANK BOOK

	Receipts				Payments				
Date	Details	Paying-in reference	Bank amount	Date	Details	Payment number	Cheque number	Bank amount	
1 Jan	Opening balance		0	10 Jan	Rent of premises	5	1701	2,500	o/s
10 Jan	Cash to bank (grant paid in)	856	7,000 ✓	11 Jan	Medical supplies	6	1702	3,000	✓
10 Jan	Sale of drugs	857	20 ✓	16 Jan	Purchase of drugs	7	1703	550	✓
12 Jan	Sale of medical supplies	858	127 o/s	27 Jan	Office equipment	8	1704	100	o/s
				31 Jan	Bank charges			20	
	Total		**7,147**		**Total**			~~6,150~~	6,170

Closing balance (7,147 less ~~6,150~~ =) ~~997~~
6,170
(revised balance) 977

BANK STATEMENT

Date	Details	In	Out	Balance
1 Jan	Opening balance			0
10 Jan	Sundries 856	7,000		7,000
10 Jan	Sundries 857	20		7,020
14 Jan	Cheque 1702		3,000	4,020
19 Jan	Cheque 1703		550	3,470
31 Jan	Bank charges → update bank book		(20)	3,450
31 Jan	**Closing balance**			**3,450**

o/s = outstanding items

Figure 28 *Primary Health-care Programme* bank reconciliation as at 31 January, based on information in Figure 27a

	Amount	Total amount	
Bank balance at 31 January (from bank statement)		3,450	[A]
Less: cheques not yet included in the bank's records			
cheque number 1701	2,500		
cheque number 1704	100	2,600	[B: total cheques]
	Sub-total	850	[A–B]
Plus: items paid in but not yet included in the bank's records			
paying-in reference 858/12 January		127	[C]
Balance in bank book at 31 January (group's own record)		**977**	[A–B+C]

Comments on the reconciliation

- Letters, for example [A], are used to show which amounts are required for the calculation.
- The balance of 977.00, adjusted from 997.00, is shown in the bank book (Figure 27b), because the 20.00 for charges is included on the payments side on 31 January. If the bank book had been finalized and the bank statement was received in February, this adjustment could instead be made in the February bank book and then the 20.00 would be included in the bank reconciliation statement at 31 January as an addition.
- You may want to ask the bank why it has not yet credited the 127.00 to your account. (This is shown in the bank book as received on 12 January).
- Cheque 1704 will, we assume, be included in the bank's records in early February.
- Cheque 1701 does not show on the bank's records, perhaps because the person to whom you paid it has been slow in paying it into his or her account.

- Remember it may take a week (or more) for the bank to process the cheque you have written.

Rules to help you to control your bank account

There are rules which need to be observed when operating a bank account:

1. Whenever a bank account is opened, it should always be registered in the name of the group, never in the name of the leader or treasurer.
2. Arrange with your bank for all cheques written by your group to be signed by at least two named people. More than two people may be signatories.
3. Cheques should be used as much as possible in making payments, as this avoids having to hold large amounts of cash. However, cheques are not always accepted as a method of payment. In this case you will have to pay in cash.
4. You should never sign blank cheques. Signed cheques are the equivalent of cash. If you really have no alternative, make sure that the name of the payee is included, and a limit set on the amount payable. Some banks will allow you to write this on the face of a cheque (for example, 'amount not to exceed two hundred ...').
5. Any money you receive should be deposited with the bank as often as practical. This is especially important before holidays and weekends, when surplus cash should not be left on the premises.
6. Cheques not cleared through the bank within a certain time-limit (often six months) should be cancelled, and the payee may be contacted in case the cheques have been lost.
7. Cheque books should be kept in a safe or other secure place. Check through the unused cheque books occasionally, to make sure no cheques are missing.
8. Banks can be asked to query any unusual items that they notice with a senior member of staff not involved in the day-to-day accounting. This is a protection against theft.

Key points of this chapter

- Complete a bank reconciliation to agree your bank book with the bank's records. This should be completed each time you receive a bank statement, or your pass book is updated.
- A bank account should be kept in the name of the group, never in the name of an individual.
- Keep cheque books in a safe place.
- At least two named people should always sign cheques or requests for money from the account.
- Do not sign blank cheques.
- Always pay money into the bank as soon as possible.
- Ask the bank to query any unusual items.

Activities for Chapter 6 *solutions in Appendix C*

6.1 Complete the following sentences:

- A bank statement is ....

- A bank reconciliation is ....

- A bank reconciliation should be completed every
  ....

- The stages to go through in reconciling a bank statement to your own bank book are as follows:

  a. Enter any .... items in your bank book to bring it up to date.

  b. Include any .... or .... from the bank statement in your bank book.

  c. .... the items that appear in your bank book *and* in the bank's records.

  d. Construct a .... to show how the two records agree. Use all the items that are not ....

6.2 Using the information from the bank book and the bank statement in Figures 29a and 29b and the outline in Figure 30, go through the four stages of completing a bank reconciliation for *Training for Development*.

Figure 29a *Training for Development* bank book as at 31 January

RECEIPTS				PAYMENTS				
Date	Details	Paying-in reference	Bank amount	Date	Details	Payment number	Cheque number	Bank amount
1 Jan	Opening balance		0	4 Jan	Rent	P701	406781	6,000
5 Jan	'Start-up' grant	201	25,000	7 Jan	Purchase of office chairs	P702	406782	1,750
14 Jan	Grant	202	15,000	16 Jan	Water charge	P703	406783	6,670
15 Jan	Fee for training	203	480	16 Jan	Purchase of projector and screen	P704	406784	4,800
				18 Jan	Hire of training rooms	P705	406786	890
				24 Jan	Purchase of television	P706	406787	3,000
				24 Jan	Accommodation: Co-ordinator	P707	406788	400
				31 Jan	Salaries	P708	406789	3,225
	Total		**40,480**		**Total**			**26,735**

Closing balance (31 January) **13,745**

Figure 29b *Training for Development* bank statement as at 31 January

NATIONAL COMMERCIAL BANK: *Training for Development* current account				
DATE	DETAILS	IN	OUT	BALANCE
1 Jan	Opening balance			0
5 Jan	Credit	25,000		25,000
8 Jan	Cheque 406781		6,000	19,000
15 Jan	Cheque 406782		1,750	17,250
15 Jan	Credit	480		17,730
19 Jan	Cheque 406783		6,670	11,060
24 Jan	Cheque 406786		890	10,170
29 Jan	Cheque 406787		3,000	7,170
30 Jan	Bank charges		430	6,740
31 Jan	**Closing balance**			**6,740**

Figure 30 *Training for Development* bank reconciliation statement as at 31 January

	Amount	Total amount	
Bank balance at 31 January (from bank statement)		....	[A]
Less: cheques not yet included in the bank's records			
cheque number	....		
cheque number	....		
cheque number	....	....	[B: total cheques]
	Sub-total	....	[A–B]
Plus: items paid in but not yet included in the bank's records			
paying-in reference		....	[C]
Balance in bank book at 31 January (group's own record)		....	[A–B+C]

[Note: include a figure wherever there is a dotted line]

6.3   What actions would you take after preparing the reconciliation in Activity 6.2?
Actions

6.4   Figures 31a and 31b show another organization's bank
reconciliation statement, for extra practice.

Using the bank book and bank statement in Figures 31a
and 31b, complete a bank reconciliation statement as at
31 May (Figure 32b).

Help in answering

Take care! The *opening* balances in the bank book and the
bank statement are not the same. This is because there
are two cheques from a previous month which did not
go through the bank statement until the beginning of
May. Therefore a bank reconciliation statement is first
needed for the end of the previous month. The closing
bank book balance and bank statement balance on 30
April are, of course, the same as the opening balances
on 1 May. The 30 April bank reconciliation statement is
shown in Figure 32a.

Figure 31a *Northern Agricultural Programme* bank book

RECEIPTS				PAYMENTS				
Date	Details	Paying-in reference	Bank amount	Date	Details	Payment number	Cheque number	Bank amount
1 May	Opening balance		5,205	4 May	Bank to cash	P1003	4017	250
9 May	Transfer from deposit account	–	5,000	7 May	Rent (1 Jan to 30 June)	P1004	4019	4,754
29 May	Amount received from PNY	156	3,497	12 May	Repairs	P1005	4020	601
				19 May	Telephone	P1006	4021	143
				23 May	Bank charges	–	–	58
				28 May	Bank to cash	P1007	4022	300
				28 May	Salaries	P1008	4023	4,167
				28 May	Tax payment	P1009	4024	1,305
				28 May	Pension payment	P1010	4025	280
Total			13,702	Total				11,858

Closing balance (31 May) 1,844

Figure 31b *Northern Agricultural Programme* bank statement

STANDARD BANK: *Northern Agricultural Programme* current account				
DATE	**DETAILS**	**IN**	**OUT**	**BALANCE**
1 May	Opening balance			7,764
2 May	Cheque 4015		195	7,569
6 May	Cheque 4016		2,364	5,205
10 May	Cheque 4017		250	4,955
10 May	Cheque 4019		4,754	201
17 May	Cheque 4020		601	400 OD
23 May	Interest	145		255 OD
23 May	Transfer	5,000		4,745
23 May	Charges		58	4,687
28 May	Cheque 4022		300	4,387
31 May	**Closing balance**			**4,387**
OD = overdrawn amount				

Figure 32a *Northern Agricultural Programme* bank reconciliation statement as at 30 April

	Amount	Total amount	
Bank balance at 30 April (from bank statement)		7,764	[A]
Less: cheques not yet included in the bank's records (included on 2 and 6 May)			
cheque number 4015	195		
cheque number 4016	2,364	2,559	[B: total cheques]
	Sub-total	5,205	[A–B]
Plus: items paid in but not yet included in the bank's records			
paying-in reference		–	[C]
Balance in bank book at 30 April (group's own record)		**5,205**	[A–B+C]

Notes:
The cheque numbers (4015 and 4016) are before the number of the first cheque recorded in the bank book for May (4017). This shows that the two outstanding cheques relate to the previous month.

In preparing the bank reconciliation at end of the **current** month, 31 May, ignore these two outstanding cheques altogether. Indeed, if they had been presented a few days earlier the bank statement and bank book opening balances would have been exactly the same.

Figure 32b *Northern Agricultural Programme* bank reconciliation statement as at 31 May

	Amount	Total amount	
Bank balance at 31 May (from bank statement)		....	[A]
Less: cheques not yet included in the bank's records			
cheque number	....		
cheque number	....		
cheque number	....		
cheque number	....	....	[B: total cheques]
	Sub-total	....	[A–B]
Plus: items paid in but not yet included in the bank's records			
paying-in reference		....	[C]
Balance in bank book at 31 May (group's own record)		....	[A–B+C]

[Note: include a figure where there is a dotted line]

6.5   What questions would you ask about the information shown in Activity 6.4?

6.6   Which of the answers a–d is the most appropriate for each of the following questions? State the reason why you have chosen this answer.

1. **A group's bank account should be opened in the name of:**
   a. All of its members
   b. The treasurer
   c. The person who opens the account
   d. The group

   Reason ....

2. **The group's bank should be told that all cheques must be signed by:**
   a. One officer of the group on his/her own
   b. The treasurer on his/her own
   c. At least two named people together
   d. The most senior person available, along with the treasurer

   Reason ....

3. **Cheques should always be used instead of cash wherever possible because:**
   a. Cash is difficult to obtain
   b. It avoids having to hold a large amount of cash on the premises

c. Cheques are much easier

d. It is important to keep the bank happy

Reason ....

4. Blank cheques should not be signed because:

a. They are the equivalent of cash and could be misused

b. The cashier may not know the amount, which is put in later

c. The bank would complain

d. The auditor would complain

Reason ....

CHAPTER 7

Summarizing the accounts

At the end of the financial year you will need to give a summary of your transactions to those who have given you money. You will also need this to present to your group or management committee. A receipts and payments account can be prepared from the cash and bank book records. This chapter shows how to present this and the information to include in it. It shows how to summarize money received and then payments, and how to pull all the information together using the same structure as included in the budget.

Keywords: summarizing the accounts; receipts and payments account; basic year-end accounting statement; example of receipts and payments account; notes to the receipts and payments account

You are now able to complete your cash and bank books, and reconcile your bank statements. Next, you will want to summarize what you have received and what you have paid. Your group will need this information, and you may want to give it to a donor too. The next two chapters will show you how to complete such a summary.

Receipts

Firstly, we will look at the receipts recorded in the cash and bank books in Figure 33.

http://dx.doi.org/10.3362/9781780448206.007

All the items need to be summarized, except for the 'cash' received into the bank on 10 January. There is a similar entry on the payments side of the cash book for 7,000.00, described as 'cash to bank' in Figure 35. These two entries will cancel each other out, and therefore neither needs to be included in the summary. This makes sense, because the only change is *where* the money is held. It was cash, and now it is in the bank. There has been no new money received or paid.

We can see from the information available that this item refers to the 7,000.00 cash received as a grant from the Department of Health on 9 January. We will include the original receipt of 7,000.00 from the cash book in the summary.

In summarizing the receipts, the categories are described as in the original budget:

- grants received (donor and Department of Health);
- miscellaneous sales.

The receipts summary will appear as in Figure 34. There are several points to note in this summary:

- The 'opening balance' figure for cash and bank is included as a 'receipt' of money, even though this is held at the beginning of the period.
- If there are several grants, you could put in one figure to summarize them. However, it is better to list them separately, as donors like their names to be shown. The miscellaneous sales include sales of drugs and medical supplies. You may prefer to show each of these separately.

If you are using an analysed cash and bank book, you can use the total at the bottom of each of the analysed columns as the figure to include in the summary.

In reality, a group or larger organization is likely to have more items than are shown here, but the following rules apply whenever you summarize receipts:

- Start off with the total of your opening cash and bank book balances.
- Summarize the items in the same order as the budget.
- Sub-divide the categories to give extra information.

Figure 33 Cash book receipts and bank book receipts

CASH BOOK RECEIPTS

Date	Details	Receipt number	Cash amount
1 Jan	Opening balance		1,000.00
3 Jan	Grant from donor	500	9,500.00
9 Jan	Grant from Dept of Health	501	7,000.00
9 Jan	Sale of drugs	502	14.50
	Total		**17,514.50**

BANK BOOK RECEIPTS

Date	Details	Paying-in reference	Bank amount
1 Jan	Opening balance		0
10 Jan	Cash to bank (grant paid in)	856	7,000.00
10 Jan	Sale of drugs	857	20.00
12 Jan	Sale of medical supplies	858	127.00
	Total		**7,147.00**

Figure 34 Summary of receipts

RECEIPTS	Amount	Total amount
Opening balance (cash/bank) 1 January		1,000.00
Grants received		
Donor	9,500.00	
Dept of Health	7,000.00	
Miscellaneous sales	161.50	
		16,661.50
Total receipts		17,661.50

Payments

Now let us look at the summary of the payments. An example is shown in Figure 36.

The 7,000.00 from 'cash to bank' in the cash book payments on 10 January will be excluded from the summary. It also appears on the receipts side of the bank book, and the entries cancel each other.

In January no cheques have been written to obtain cash. If there were any, they would not have been included in the summary of receipts and payments. This is because money would only be transferred from the bank account into cash. No money would have changed hands. The only difference would be *where* the money is held.

The main categories of payments are for:

- salaries;
- rent of premises;
- purchase of drugs;
- medical supplies;
- office expenses.

These are the same as the budget headings shown in Figure 1. There is a heading for 'electricity' in the budget, but nothing has yet been paid against it.

Figure 35 Cash book and bank book payments

	CASH BOOK PAYMENTS		
Date	Details	Payment number	Cash amount
3 Jan	Stationery for office	1	10.00
5 Jan	Purchase of medical supplies	2	650.00
7 Jan	Driver's salary	3	200.00
7 Jan	Purchase of drugs	4	3,450.00
10 Jan	Cash to bank (grant paid in)	—	7,000.00
	Total		**11,310.00**

	BANK BOOK PAYMENTS		
Date	Details	Paying-in reference	Bank amount
10 Jan	Rent of premises	5	0
11 Jan	Cash to bank (grant paid in)	6	7,000.00
16 Jan	Medical supplies	7	20.00
27 Jan	Purchase of drugs	8	127.00
	Total		**7,147.00**

Figure 36 Summary of payments

PAYMENTS	Amount	Total amount
Salaries	200.00	
Rent of premises	2,500.00	
Purchase of drugs	4,000.00	
Medical supplies	3,650.00	
Electricity	—	
Office expenses	110.00	
Total payments		10,460.00
Closing balance (cash/bank), 31 January		**7,201.50**

The summary of payments would, therefore, look like Figure 36.

You will see that the payments summary has a figure included for the 'closing balance' (cash/bank) on 31 January. This should agree with the amount of cash held at that date, plus the balance in the bank book (which has been agreed with the bank statement or pass book). This will be used as the opening balance figure in the following month's accounts.

This summary of the receipts and payments is usually prepared at the end of the year (or end of a project period). The summary is called a **receipts and payments account.** It shows what has happened to your cash and bank items, and gives an overall picture of what you have received and paid.

Whenever this kind of summary is used, the heading will say that it is a receipts and payments account, and it will state the name of the group involved, and the period of time that it covers.

Putting it all together

Figure 37 shows a presentation of the whole account.

The columns in this example are merely to provide a sub-total of the information. By having the individual receipts in the left column, we are able to produce a total receipts figure in the right column [B]. The same is true for the payments [C]. This allows us to add or subtract one figure at a time in the right column.

Receipts and payments accounts should be presented with the same main headings as in your budget. This makes comparisons easier, as we will see in Chapter 9. Also, make sure that the 'closing balance' is underlined (as shown in Figure 37: **7,201.50**). This helps to highlight the amount of money held at the end of the period.

It is usual, and important, to add notes to the receipts and payments account to explain the reasons for what has happened. These are discussed in Chapter 9 and the example of the notes shown in Figure 44 could equally well be included after this receipts and payments account. An example of another organization's receipts and payments account, with notes included, is shown in Appendix A.

This receipts and payments account is only for the month of January, to cover the information shown. It is more usual for a receipts and payments account to be presented at the end of the financial year or project period.

Figure 37 Example of a receipts and payments account

Primary Health-care Programme: receipts and payments account for the period 1 to 31 January 20--			
	Amount	Total amount	
RECEIPTS			
Opening balance, 1 January		1,000.00	[A]
Grants received			
Donor	9,500.00		
Dept of Health	7,000.00		
Miscellaneous sales	161.50		
Total receipts		16,661.50	[B: total receipts]
		17,661.50	[A+B]
PAYMENTS			
Salaries	200.00		
Rent of premises	2,500.00		
Purchase of drugs	4,000.00		
Medical supplies	3,650.00		
Electricity	–		
Office expenses	110.00		
Total payments		10,460.00	[C: total payments]
Closing balance, 31 January		**7,201.50**	[A+B–C]

[The letters A, B and C are included to show where the calculations are made. These would not normally be shown in a receipts and payments account.]

Key points of this chapter

- Summarize your accounts by preparing a receipts and payments account, usually at the end of the year or project period.
- Include the receipts and the payments under the same headings as used in the budget.
- If cash is paid into the bank account, exclude these items from the summary. The same applies when cash is withdrawn from the bank.
- If the budget heading includes several items, sub-divide them to give more information.
- Include the total cash/bank book balances at the beginning and end of the period covered.
- Remember to give the summary a title: receipts and payments account, the name of the group or project, and the period covered.
- Notes can be added to the account to provide additional information.

Activities for Chapter 7 *solutions in Appendix C*

7.1   The receipts side of an analysed cash and bank book for January is shown in Figure 38. Using Figure 39 and the analysed cash and bank book analysis columns in Figure 38, prepare the *receipts* part of the receipts and payments account. Include all the items here even though some have a nil balance.

Note: the receipts and payments account would often be produced at the end of the financial year or project period rather than monthly.

Figure 38 *Training for Development analysed cash and bank book – receipts side*

Date	Details	Receipt number	Paying-in reference	Cash amount	Bank amount	Opening balance	Grants from donors	Fees for training	Sale of materials	Other receipts
1 Jan	Opening balance			0	0	0				
1 Jan	Fees for training	1		1,300				1,300		
4 Jan	Fees for training	2		2,800				2,800		
5 Jan	'Start-up' grant		201		25,000		25,000			
10 Jan	Sale of booklet	3		25					25	
14 Jan	Grant		202		15,000		15,000			
15 Jan	Fees for training		203		480			480		
15 Jan	Fees for training	4		1,350				1,350		
20 Jan	Sale of materials	5		15					15	
27 Jan	Sale of booklet	6		25					25	
	Total			**5,515**	**40,480**	**0**	**40,000**	**5,930**	**65**	**0**

Figure 39 *Training for Development receipts side of receipts and payments account*

RECEIPTS	Amount	Total amount
Opening balance bank/cash, 1 January	....	
	....	
	....	
	....	
	....	
Total receipts		....

7.2 The payments side of the analysed cash and bank book is shown in Figure 41. Using Figure 40, and the information in Figure 41, prepare the payments part of the receipts and payments account. Again, include all the items. You may wish to identify separately some items that are grouped together in the analysed cash and bank book, to provide more information.

Figure 40 *Training for Development* payments side of receipts and payments account

PAYMENTS	Amount	Total amount
	....	
	....	
	....	
	....	
	....	
	....	
	....	
	....	
	....	
	....	
	....	
	....	
	....	
	....	
	....	
	....	
Total payments		....
Closing balance bank/cash, 31 January		....

Figure 41 *Training for Development* analysed cash and bank book – payments side

Date	Details	Payment number	Cheque number	Cash amount	Bank amount	Salaries	Rent/electricity/water telephone	Training materials	Office expenses (incl. audit)	Travel/accommodation	Hire of training rooms	Office/training equipment	Other payments
4 Jan	Rent	P701	406781		6,000		6,000						
4 Jan	Purchase of stationery	P1		400					400				
4 Jan	Purchase of desks	P2		1,000								1,000	
7 Jan	Photocopying	P3		200					200				
7 Jan	Purchase of office chairs	P702	406782		1,750							1,750	
7 Jan	Purchase of training materials	P4		900				900					
9 Jan	Purchase of stationery	P5		250					250				
10 Jan	Hire of training rooms	P6		400							400		
14 Jan	Purchase of filing cabinet	P7		700								700	
16 Jan	Water charge	P703	406783		6,670		6,670						
16 Jan	Purchase of projector and screen	P704	406784		4,800							4,800	
18 Jan	Hire of training rooms	P705	406786		890						890		
19 Jan	Travel: Co-ordinator	P8		320						320			
24 Jan	Purchase of television	P706	406787		3,000							3,000	
24 Jan	Accommodation: Co-ordinator	P707	406788		400					400			
25 Jan	Purchase of small office items	P9		240					240				
31 Jan	Salaries	P708	406789		3,225	3,225							
	Total			**4,410**	**26,735**	**3,225**	**12,670**	**900**	**1,090**	**720**	**1,290**	**11,250**	**0**

Closing balance (31 January)

1,105   13,745

7.3   Using the space provided in Figure 42, present the
          receipts and payments account in full, with:

- the name of the organization, a title, and period
  covered by the account;
- a correct format for a receipts and payments account.

Figure 42 *Training for Development* receipts and payments account

	Amount	Total amount

CHAPTER 8

Summarizing the accounts with more information

When you have prepared a receipts and payments account, there are a number of steps that can be taken to provide more information. This can be useful for your own organization or group, but also for other users of the account. These include amounts that you have paid in advance, or that are outstanding and due to you at the end of the year. You need to explain these items at the end of the receipts and payments account. The chapter shows how to identify, for example, any purchased items that will last for more than one year. Guidance is also given about how to add explanatory notes to the account.

Keywords: notes to the receipts and payments account; basic year-end accounting statement; summarizing the accounts; saving money to replace items bought; accounting for amounts paid in advance

The previous chapter showed how to put together a receipts and payments account. It is a useful way of summarizing all the money that has come in and gone out. However, there are some limitations. This chapter will show you some steps to improve the usefulness of the receipts and payments account.

http://dx.doi.org/10.3362/9781780448206.008

How to improve the receipts and payments account

Amounts paid in advance, or owed by you

The receipts and payments account gives you a summary of all items. It does not tell you how they relate to a specific period of time. For example, if the electricity charge for January were paid in February, it would not appear in the January account, so it would look as though no electricity had been used. There are two ways of avoiding this:

- Try to avoid having items outstanding at the point when you prepare the receipts and payments account for the year-end. In practice this is not easy, but one way to keep amounts to the minimum is by paying invoices for the period before the date of the receipts and payments account. Also, try to make sure that as many as possible of the amounts owed to the group are collected before that date.
- Keep a record of any items that are outstanding at the end of a period, and include the total for that budget item as a note at the bottom of the receipts and payments account. An example of this kind of note can be seen in Figure 44.

Saving money to replace items that will wear out

It is important to save for the eventual replacement of items such as equipment, vehicles, or machinery. Each month (or less frequently if you prefer), put aside some money towards the cost of replacing each item. Pay this into a savings or deposit account and create a separate 'savings account' bank book in your own records.

The transfer will be shown as a payment out of your 'current account' bank book, and as a receipt into your 'savings account' bank book. In the receipts and payments account the transfer will appear as a payment, but a note at the bottom of the account should show that this account is for replacements. Any interest gained can be added to the 'savings account' to help offset increasing costs.

How much should you set aside? You could divide up the cost of the item by the number of months it is likely to last. For example, you could say that a computer, which originally cost 480.00, will last four years. So you would put 10.00 per month (480.00 divided by 48 months) into a savings account over each of the four years.

However, with ever-increasing prices, it is likely that in four years' time a computer will cost more than 480.00, and you would not have enough money to replace it. The amount to be set aside each month depends on the circumstances, the life of the item, the rate of inflation, and, for international purchases, the exchange rate. As a guide, an amount based on double the original cost may be appropriate.

Your group, or the donor funding the programme, may say it is not possible to put money aside in this way. If so, you need to ask yourself what will happen when the item is no longer usable. You may feel that the only way to replace it would be to ask for a further grant or to arrange additional fundraising. If the future of the group depends on an item – for example, a vehicle – arrangements should be made well in advance, and not left until an item is beyond repair.

Separating longer-term items from day-to-day expenses

The receipts and payments account treats all expenditure in the same way. It will not be obvious in the summary if a large amount has been spent on items that you intend to keep for a long time, such as furniture and equipment. (Such items are sometimes called **fixed assets**.) So you should make a note of such purchases at the end of the account. An example for a full year is shown in Figure 43.

Figure 43 A record of fixed assets appended to a receipts and payments account

Fixed assets bought during the year:	
	Cost
Office equipment	890.00
Furniture	1,655.00
Total	**2,545.00**

Has a surplus been made?

The receipts and payments account may show how you are doing in terms of cash or bank balance available, but it will not show whether you have made a surplus or a deficit. For this, a further account summary would be needed, which may require the help of a professional accountant.

Additional notes

In the receipts and payments account (Figure 37), some of the items would have been explained further if additional notes had been added. The notes needed for this example are added to the summary shown in Figure 44.

Another example of a receipts and payments account for a full year, with notes and comparative figures for the previous year, is shown in Appendix A.

Key points of this chapter

- Keep a list of any items outstanding at the date of your receipts and payments account, and include a note of them at the end of the account.
- It is important to set aside money for the eventual replacement of longer-term items.
- This money should be put into a savings or deposit account each month.

- The calculation of the correct amount will depend on the inflation and exchange rates and the expected life of the item.
- Show in a note how much has been spent on items with a life of more than a year.
- The receipts and payments account will show you the cash/ bank position, but not the surplus or deficit that your group has made.
- Additional notes to the receipts and payments account will further explain the items included.

The receipts and payments account will produce a summarized statement at the end of the accounting period. When a group starts to grow (for example, when it has a number of employees or owns vehicles and equipment), it will need to consider preparing a more complex financial summary. Such accounts are, however, outside the scope of this book. If they are needed, further help should be sought from an professional accountant.

Activities for Chapter 8 *solutions in Appendix C*

8.1   What are some of the limitations of the receipts and payments account? How might you overcome these limitations?

   a. Limitation:

       How to overcome:

   b. Limitation:

       How to overcome:

   c. Limitation:

       How to overcome:

8.2   How can money be saved to replace items that will wear out?

CHAPTER 9

Providing the information your group needs

In addition to the year-end receipts and payments account, your organization or group will need to know about its financial position throughout the year. This chapter shows how to use this information to identify whether any changes are needed to your plans, for example to raise more money or to spend less. Examples show how to compare the budget for the accounting period under review (perhaps the previous three months) with the actual receipts received and payments paid. It shows how to prepare accompanying notes to the 'budget and actual statement', to highlight the current financial position. Examples demonstrate how to prepare statements showing the financial position from the beginning of the year to date (the 'cumulative budget and actual statement').

Keywords: budget and actual statement; interpreting budget and actual statements; regular internal financial reporting; internal management of community organizations and small groups; asking questions about the budget and actual figures

One of the reasons why a group should keep accounts is to have an accurate record of its financial transactions. Another is to be able to use this information to manage and improve the group's activities. Good use of financial information is often the key to a group's success or failure.

http://dx.doi.org/10.3362/9781780448206.009

When queries arise, the information in the cash and bank books will help to answer them. Start there, and if the entry in the book itself does not help, the references to supporting documents will tell you where to find more information.

How much money is left?

The cash and bank books will tell you if you have enough money to pay your expenses. You need to look at the cash book regularly, to make sure that you do not run out of cash. Likewise, the bank book will show what is left in the bank account. If you are likely to run out of money altogether (use the cash-flow forecast to help you predict this), you must alert the people responsible for running the group as soon as possible. If this is not done, the whole programme could be in danger of failing.

Regular reporting

When we looked at budgeting in Chapter 2, we said that in addition to making the overall budget it was helpful to divide it up, showing what money would be available month by month (Figure 2).

Looking again at our example of a primary health-care programme, we will prepare a summary for January, comparing what was planned with what has actually been received or paid. This is referred to as a **budget and actual statement**. It uses the same headings as the budget (Figure 44).

Figure 44 includes the following columns:

Item: a listing of the budget headings for receipts and payments.

Note: a reference to additional information at the bottom of the table. It is important to inform users of the reasons for differences between budgeted and actual figures.

Budgeted amount for January: the proportion of the budget that is expected to be received or paid in the first month.

Amount received/spent in January: actual receipts and payments in January, which can be compared with the budget to see whether there are differences.

Difference: the overspend on payments and the under-collection of budgeted receipts.

Figure 44 Example of a budget and actual statement with notes

Item	Note	Budgeted amount for January	Amount received/ spent in January	Difference
RECEIPTS				
Grants received				
Donor		9,500.00	9,500.00	0.00
Dept of Health	2	14,000.00	7,000.00	(7,000.00)
Miscellaneous sales		50.00	161.50	111.50
Total receipts		**23,550.00**	**16,661.50**	**(6,888.50)**
PAYMENTS				
Salaries		1,000.00	200.00	800.00
Rent of premises	3	417.00	2,500.00	(2,083.00)
Purchase of drugs		5,000.00	4,000.00	1,000.00
Medical supplies	4	4,400.00	3,650.00	750.00
Electricity	5	83.00	–	83.00
Office expenses	4	310.00	110.00	200.00
Total payments		**11,210.00**	**10,460.00**	**750.00**
Total difference		**12,340.00**	**6,201.50**	**(6,138.50)**

Notes:

1. **Amounts in brackets** ( ) show negative differences – an overspend on payments and an under-collection of budgeted receipts.
2. **The Department of Health** grant was to have been paid in two instalments; it will now be paid in four instalments.
3. **Rent of premises** has been paid in January for the six months from January to June.
4. **Fixed assets** bought during January:

	Cost
Medical supplies	
Medical equipment	1,250.00
Total	**1,250.00**
Office expenses	
Office equipment	100.00
Total	**100.00**

5. **Electricity** is due to be paid in March. It is estimated that 95.00 is owed for January.
6. **Amounts held in cash and bank:**

	Amount
Balance held in cash 31 Jan.	6,204.50
Balance in current account 31 Jan.	997.00
Total	**7,201.50**

This final column highlights the main differences and shows where to concentrate your effort to make sure that you keep to the budget. These details for this example are shown in the section headed 'What does the statement show?'.

Notes like those that are also needed at the end of the receipts and payments account (explained in Chapter 7) are included in Figure 44, to give more information. These notes are an essential explanation of the reason for the differences between the budgeted amounts and the actual amounts received or spent.

This type of report, with its regular breakdown, gives an overall picture of the group's finances, which will be needed by group members, or the management committee.

What does the statement show?

- Showing negative differences in brackets helps to draw users' attention to the figures that may cause concern.
- The statement shows that the group has received significantly less than expected in the budget, mainly because the Department of Health grant is now being received in four instalments, rather than two. This could have serious consequences for the group, but it seems that the money was not in fact all needed in January. You will need to consult and amend the cash-flow forecast to see what effect this will have on future months.
- The fact that rent was paid in January for six months in advance may mean that the group will run short of cash. Again, consult the cash-flow forecast.
- One of the reasons for the overspending of rent may be that costs have increased. If this is the case for a specific item, or if the increase distorts the figures, it is important to draw attention to the fact in a note explaining what has happened.
- Note 4 shows that medical equipment and office equipment, longer-term items, have been purchased. It is worth asking if these items were included in the budget. If not, less money will be available for planned expenditure, and it

will be necessary to decide on the highest priorities. Ideally long-term items should be identified separately in the budget.

- Always look closely at what has actually happened, and keep asking questions. If there is a difference, always check whether it has been caused by timing (if receipts have come in or payments have gone out earlier or later than you had planned), or whether it is an activity that you had not planned at all. If so, ask what will be done about it.

- This monthly report will be important when your organization takes policy decisions, so be sure that the information is as accurate and up to date as possible.

- A column for the percentage difference between the 'budget' and 'actual' figures could be added to highlight major variations.

It is important to produce a summary like the one in Figure 44 regularly, so that everyone can see the financial situation. Encourage the management committee, especially, to ask questions about financial information.

Reporting from the beginning of the year to date

In addition to the monthly report shown in Figure 44, it is useful to present a report for the months from the beginning of the financial year to date. This is sometimes called a **cumulative budget and actual report**. The **cumulative total** is the current month's figure, plus the total from all previous months of the financial year. In January, or whenever your year starts, there would, however, be only one month to report on. The headings for such a report at the end of March would look like those in Figure 45.

Figure 45 Headings for a cumulative budget and actual statement, January–March

Item	Note	Budget: March	Amount received/ spent: March	Difference	Budget: Jan–Mar	Amount received/ spent: Jan–Mar	Difference

Key points of this chapter

- The information in the accounts is important to the running of any group.
- Make use of the cash book and bank book to answer queries.
- Know how much money you have left in cash and/or at the bank.
- Present your budget and actual statement regularly to the group or its management committee.
- Add notes to the statement to give more information.
- Include a similar report from the beginning of the year to date (a cumulative budget and actual statement).
- Be critical, and keep asking questions about anything in the statement that you do not understand. Encourage others to ask questions too.

Activities for Chapter 9 *solutions in Appendix C*

9.1   Using Figure 46, prepare a budget and actual statement for *Training for Development* for the month of January. Use the figures for January from Figure 4 in Activity 2.2 and the 'actuals' from the analysed cash and bank book totals in Activity 5.4.

You will notice that, in order to find the required figure for this statement, some amounts will need to be added together, and others should be separated out.

Figure 46 *Training for Development* budget and actual statement for January 20--

Item	Note	Budgeted amount for January	Amount received/spent in January	Difference
RECEIPTS				
Dept of Education 'start-up' grant				
Grants received from donors				
Fees for training				
Sale of materials				
Total receipts				
PAYMENTS				
Salaries				
Office rent				
Electricity/water/telephone				
Training materials				
Office expenses (including audit)				
Travel/accommodation				
Hire of training rooms				
Office equipment				
Training equipment				
Total payments				
Total difference				

9.2 Explain the reasons why the 'difference' column has a negative figure for receipts, when less is received than budgeted; but a positive figure for payments, when less is spent than budgeted. How can the negative figures help interpret the statement?

9.3 *Training for Development* has not made an entry for a 'transfer to a savings account'. If it had, where would the entry appear in the statement shown in Activity 9.1?

9.4 Add notes to the budget and actual statement for January, based on the following headings:

Office and training equipment

Amounts held in cash and bank

Information to help with these notes will be found in Activity 5.4.

9.5 As a member of the management committee of *Training for Development,* what questions would you ask about the budget and actual statement for January shown in Figure 46?

CHAPTER 10

Having the accounts checked

Having the accounts checked is an important way to confirm that the group has used its money correctly, and that it is trustworthy. This chapter explains the process of 'audit' or 'examination' of the accounting by considering who is appointed to check the accounts, what happens when the accounts are checked, and what records will be required as part of the process. It considers the reports that auditors provide – firstly the audit report, which is a brief summary saying whether the auditor/examiner has concerns; and secondly a 'management letter', which gives more detailed information of group practices that could be improved.

Keywords: audit; independent examination; independent review; management letter; audit report; documents required for an audit or independent examination

The work of the person who keeps a group's accounts must always be checked by another person, at least once a year. In this way, mistakes can be found and corrected, and the person who is keeping the accounts can prove that she or he is honest. This type of check is called an **examination, review** or **audit**, and the person carrying it out is called an **examiner, reviewer** or **auditor**.

http://dx.doi.org/10.3362/9781780448206.010

Who is appointed to check the accounts?

It is most important that the person who is appointed as examiner or auditor should be independent. Sometimes the person checking the accounts is called an **independent examiner** or **independent reviewer**. The person must not be involved in the keeping of the accounts, or be related to any of the group leaders. The person should be respected, and able to communicate with people well. He or she should have some knowledge of book-keeping, and ideally be a qualified accountant. In some countries it is a legal requirement to have a qualified accountant or auditor. The examiner or auditor may require a fee or payment, and donors are often willing to pay for this – but do not forget to include this item in your budget!

What happens when the accounts are checked?

The examination/audit will usually take place once a year, soon after the end of the period covered by your accounts. The examiner/auditor will want to count your cash, and will ask to see the following records:

- cash book and bank book;
- receipts for money coming in and payments going out;
- invoices;
- information from donors;
- any correspondence about the group, and especially about the accounting;
- bank statements or pass books;
- cheque books and old cheque 'stubs', paying-in slips/books;
- bank reconciliations, especially for the year-end;
- budget and actual statements;
- receipts and payments account;
- a record of group meetings;
- staff records;
- a list of items owned; for example, vehicles, equipment, and furniture.

The examiner/auditor will inspect these and other documents in detail, and will ask questions to clarify the information. She or he will also ask for information about the way in which the group is run.

After the examination/audit, a detailed letter will often be written to the leader of the group or to the management committee to say what has been done (this is sometimes called a **management letter**). The letter may suggest ways to improve the accounts and the group management as a whole. This can be very useful, and it may help you to make your group's activities more effective.

Finally, the examiner/auditor will 'sign the accounts' (usually a copy of the receipts and payments account) to say they are correct. They may also write an **audit report** that confirms that they have conducted the examination or audit. If there are any serious items of concern this may be included in the audit report. In this case, the examiner/auditor should have discussed this with the group's leader beforehand. This report should form part of the final accounting statements. Copies of these statements may then be sent to anyone who is interested. It is good practice to display the audit report and the receipts and payments account on your website, if you have one.

If the term 'audit' is used for the checking of the accounts, this is likely to imply a more formal inspection of the accounts and sometimes it is required by law.

Other checks

In addition to the annual examination/audit, other people may want to see your accounts for themselves. It is good practice to agree to such requests. It will help to maintain a good relationship with people who are likely to give you money in the future. In reality, however, if an examination/audit has already been carried out, many people will be happy to accept a copy of the signed receipts and payments account.

Key points of this chapter

- An independent examiner/auditor must be appointed to check the accounts.
- He or she should have some knowledge of book-keeping, or be a qualified accountant.
- The inspection should take place soon after the period covered by your accounts, and all records should be made available on request.
- A management letter is likely to be written, with recommendations for improving the group's financial management.
- The receipts and payments account should be signed to say that the examination/audit has taken place.
- Other people may want to inspect your accounts. Welcome them!

Activities for Chapter 10 *solutions in Appendix C*

10.1 What is the most important quality of an examiner/ auditor of a group's accounts?

10.2 List the records the examiner/auditor will expect to see when conducting an examination/audit of a group's accounts.

10.3 What is the purpose of a management letter?

10.4 What might be the consequences of not having your accounts examined or audited?

CHAPTER 11

Relations with donors

People who give money ('donors' or 'funders') play an important part in many organizations and groups. This chapter looks at the types of donor who provide funding, what accounting documents they are likely to require, and issues about reporting back for money received. It also looks at how a small group might arrange its accounting to make the most of the information it has already produced and avoid extra work when reporting to different donors.

Keywords: donors/funders; how to approach donors/funders; accounting requirements of donors/funders; reporting to donors/funders; accounting building blocks to make donor/funder reporting easier

Many groups rely on external funders to provide money to help them to carry out their programmes. This chapter looks at the ways in which groups relate to these funders, or **donors**. Each donor's requirements are different. This chapter will therefore provide some general points which apply to the majority of donors.

Who are the donors?

Those organizations described as donors fall into a number of categories:

- international non-government organizations (INGOs), for example the Aga Khan Foundation, Concern, Oxfam;

http://dx.doi.org/10.3362/9781780448206.011

- national non-government organizations (NGOs), for example Sudanaid, Thaicraft;
- trusts and foundations;
- national embassies;
- religious groups;
- companies or local businesses;
- individual people.

Some of these donors are themselves funded by large international agencies, such as:

- United Nations organizations, for example UN High Commissioner for Refugees (UNHCR), UN Children's Fund (UNICEF);
- government or inter-government agencies, for example Danida (Denmark), the Indian Government, the European Union.

These large donors which fund, for example, INGOs may create a 'chain of funding'. The INGO may fund a national NGO, local NGO, or community-based organization (CBO) directly. All donors demand a high standard of accounting from the groups that they fund. If, for example, a government donor is funding a CBO through an INGO, the accounting of the CBO must be of a high standard to allow the INGO to fully account back to the government. If the INGO cannot account adequately, it may have to refund the money.

Approaches to donors

The first stage of applying to a particular donor is to discover the types of programme that they are likely to fund. Most donors will produce written details, available on request or shown on their website. If other similar groups have already worked with a particular donor it is helpful to talk with them and discover the types of programme likely to be funded.

It is important to understand each donor's way of operating. Most will request information about your group. It is polite to send this quickly and to send additional information regularly (for example, newsletters and annual reports).

If changes occur, for example a delay in the start of a programme, you should keep the donor informed. This contact will often lead to an agreement, for example to extend the length of the programme. However, the donor may refuse to fund a programme because it is not the one they had originally approved. If you are unhappy with the donor's decision, it is acceptable to negotiate with them. If you would like to do something different from what they are offering, talk with them about this.

Any communication to or from donors should be recorded in writing, and copies should be kept on file. These written records are essential for future reference, especially when the people who made the original agreement are replaced by new members of staff.

Accounting requirements

An application for funding will usually include a budget, with notes of detailed calculations and a written description of the programme. You may also be required to give a justification for individual items within the budget. Some donors provide their own application forms, listing their requirements.

When an agreement to fund is given, there will usually be a **letter of agreement** or **contract**. This will give details of the following items:

Reporting requirements

The frequency of reporting back to the donor will be stated. The letter will show deadlines for reports (often six monthly and at the end of the year); these should be strictly followed.

Tendering and purchasing

The letter may indicate the rules for tendering and purchasing of goods and services. It is likely to say that, where possible, three quotes should be obtained for larger purchases, for example vehicles. It may also state what will happen to these items at the end of the programme.

Auditing

Donors may require their own annual audit, although usually a copy of the annual accounting statements, independently examined or audited, will be sufficient. It is essential to keep all accounting documentation relating to the programme for at least seven years, or longer if required by national law.

All changes to the programme must be agreed in advance by the donor. If not, the donor may be unwilling to fund anything not included in the original budget. The donor should agree all changes in writing.

Building blocks of accounting

The systems described in this book will form the basis of what a group needs in order to monitor its own financial management. When donors are involved, however, this may become more complicated. While some donors expect only to receive a copy of the annual accounting statements, others may ask the group to provide a budget, and to report on actual receipts and payments, in the donor's own format. This may be different from what the group has prepared for its own purposes.

Indeed, if there are several donors, each one may ask for something rather different. It is important therefore when designing the budget for a group to be aware of what donors are likely to require, thus avoiding extra work in the future. Try to use the budget items as 'building blocks' so that they provide the data required and thus make reporting easier. This may mean that items are broken down further than would otherwise be the case, in order to report in the format requested by a donor.

For example, if a donor agrees to fund part of the annual drugs budget, all invoices connected with purchases may have to be presented at the year-end. It may then be worth breaking the drugs budget into two parts, rather than one, so that the information is classified separately throughout the year. This avoids having the time-consuming task of re-analysing expenditure at the end of the year.

It is often worth seeking advice on establishing such a system at the beginning of a donor's involvement, particularly where a significant amount of funding is received, or complex activities are funded.

Reporting to people who have given you money

A financial report will normally be sent regularly (usually every three to six months) to organizations which have given you money. Each donor will require something slightly different but their requirements will often include:

- the receipts and payments account (or other accounting statements outside the scope of this book) for the period to which the amount relates (at the end of the funding period);
- an examiner's or auditor's statement (at the end of the funding period);
- the cumulative budget and actual statement for the period;
- copies of (or original) invoices (some donors instead require the right to audit the accounts);
- if money was given for a particular purpose, details of how the individual donation has been spent, and a note to say how much money is left over;
- an explanation of any changes to this year's budget;
- a budget for next year, if funding is to continue.

It is sometimes difficult to know what to do with money that has not been spent for the purpose it was given. Some donors will ask for such amounts to be returned to them while others may permit it to be used for other parts of the programme. It is worth discussing this with the donor if you expect that there will be money left over; if it is appropriate, you might propose a way of using these excess funds.

Increases in workload

Requesting and receiving additional funding can often create more work, both for the programme staff and the accounting staff.

If the funding is likely to enlarge the group's activities significantly, it is worth looking again at the accounting requirement before the funds are requested. There will be additional transactions, extra budgeting, and extra work involved in reporting back to donors. There is often a need to review financial systems more generally, in order to respond to the high standards demanded by donors. It may be necessary to recruit a finance officer or to give further training of existing staff. This can be justified if large additional amounts are involved; a donor may be willing to fund an extra person. It may be necessary to ask a qualified accountant to provide advice.

Key points of this chapter

- There is a wide variety of donors, but all will require a high standard of accounting.
- It is wise to talk with other groups who have worked with a particular donor.
- Keep donors informed about any changes to the programme; retain copies of all correspondence relating to such changes.
- It is acceptable to negotiate with donors.
- Donors will produce a contract or letter of agreement to formalize the arrangement, containing details of how and when to report back, rules about tendering and purchasing, and information about accounting and audit.
- Break down the original budget in a way that will enable you to report to donors in the format required. If in doubt, seek advice.
- Send regular reports to your donors. Talk with donors about the use of surplus donor funds.
- Accepting donors' funds may lead to an increase in workload for those producing accounting information. Seek advice about the need for changes in staffing or in financial systems.

Activities for Chapter 11 *solutions in Appendix C*

11.1 Complete the following sentences in relation to donors:

- All donors require a .... from groups they fund.
- The first stage of applying to a particular donor is to discover ....
- When changes occur, ...
- Any correspondence with donors should be ....

11.2 Which of the answers a–d is the most appropriate for each of the following questions? State the reason why you have chosen this answer.

1. **When donors are involved in funding the purchase of a new vehicle, they are likely to ask for:**
   a. Photographs of the vehicle
   b. Three quotes from suppliers to be received before a purchase is made
   c. An explanation of who will be responsible for maintaining the vehicle
   d. A record of all journeys made

   Reason...

2. **When significant extra funding is received, the effect on those who prepare the accounts may be that:**
   a. They will stop inspecting travel claims in so much detail
   b. Visits to the programme become more frequent
   c. They can take a holiday
   d. Their workload increases

   Reason...

3. **A letter of agreement between a group and a donor will usually show:**
   a. Details of when and how reports should be provided
   b. Which party is responsible if things go wrong
   c. The name of the auditor of the programme
   d. Background information about the programme

   Reason...

CHAPTER 12

Regular financial tasks

Community organizations and small groups need to carry out many regular financial tasks. This chapter lists the most important tasks to be carried out daily, weekly, monthly and yearly. It encourages users to add additional tasks to the lists that their organization or group may require.

Keywords: regular financial checks; financial checks for community organizations and small groups; financial checks for charities; financial tasks daily, weekly, monthly, yearly for organizations or groups

You will have realized from reading this book that some accounting tasks need to be performed on a regular basis. Some are completed daily or weekly, others monthly, and some yearly.

The main tasks are listed in the following checklists. You may find it helpful to tick off and date the items as you complete them. Add to the lists as you find other requirements for your own group.

http://dx.doi.org/10.3362/9781780448206.012

Daily financial tasks

	Date task completed
1. Make payments of cash.	
2. Bank all cheques received.	
3. Write down details of money coming in and going out in the cash and bank books.	
4. The cashier should agree the cash book balance with the actual cash amount.	
5. Monitor the cash balance to decide whether more is required from the bank account.	
6. Pay urgent invoices.	

Weekly financial tasks

	Date task completed
1. Arrange for a senior member of the group to check the cash book balance against the actual cash amount. (This should be done at different times each week, and the cashier should be present.)	
2. Pay outstanding invoices.	
3. Update the records of outstanding payments and amounts due. Send out invoices to people who owe you money.	

Monthly financial tasks

	Date task completed
1. Ensure that the cash book and bank book are up to date.	
2. Enter any outstanding items from the bank statements not already included in the bank book (for example, bank charges, interest, and standing orders).	
3. Prepare a bank reconciliation to agree your bank book with the bank statement (or pass book).	
4. Follow up any questions raised by this reconciliation.	
5. Examine the details of any amounts advanced to staff and ensure that they have been accounted for and/or repaid. Remind those who have not paid back their advances.	
6. Take appropriate action if people have owed you money for more than one month: send a reminder or contact them by telephone.	
7. When the monthly accounts have been completed, produce a statement of the budget, compared with actual receipts and payments. (Small groups may do this less frequently, for example every two or three months.) Add notes to this and investigate any unusual differences. The statement should be presented to the management committee.	
8. Update the cash-flow forecast and take any action needed.	
9. Provide any regular information required by donors. Make sure that donors are aware of any changes in activities that they are funding.	

Annual/year-end financial tasks

	Date task completed
1. Make sure that the cash book and bank book are completely up to date. Include items from the final month's bank statement. Prepare the bank reconciliation before the accounts are finalized.	
2. Update the records of outstanding payments and amounts due. Try to ensure that these are kept to a minimum. Prepare a list of outstanding items at the year-end.	
3. Examine any outstanding amounts advanced to staff and ensure that they have been accounted for and/or repaid before the year-end. Remind those who have not repaid their advances.	
4. Produce a final year-end budget and actual statement.	
5. Prepare the annual receipts and payments account, together with accompanying notes.	
6. Ensure that the management committee appoints an independent examiner/auditor for the accounts (in good time before the end of the year).	
7. Check that all records are filed in order, and that the documents likely to be required by the examiner/auditor are available.	
8. Consult this person about the timetable for the examination of the accounts.	
9. Follow up any points raised by the examiner/auditor. Present these, and any correspondence, to the management committee. Decide any action needed as a result of the examiner/auditor's comments.	
10. Review the financial systems/information more generally and make any necessary changes. Identify any weaknesses and find ways to improve them.	
11. Have the accounts approved by the management committee and the annual general meeting (if one is held).	
12. Ensure that the Chair of the management committee and the examiner/auditor have signed one copy of the receipts and payments account. Keep this document in a safe place.	
13. Send a copy of it, and a report of the group's activities, to donors and anyone else who might be interested.	
14. Provide any additional information required by donors.	
15. Prepare a budget and cash-flow forecast, in advance, for next year.	

	Date task completed

Key points of this chapter

- It is important to complete financial tasks methodically and at the right time.
- Daily tasks include: providing cash; making sure that the cash and bank books are updated; monitoring the cash balance; and paying urgent invoices.
- Weekly tasks include: a cash count by a senior group member; payment of outstanding invoices; and management of records of money owing and money due.
- Monthly tasks include: updating cash and bank records and preparing a bank reconciliation statement; managing money advanced and outstanding invoices; preparing a budget and actual statement; updating the cash-flow forecast; and providing information required to donors.
- Annual/year-end tasks include: updating all records and investigating outstanding advances; preparing a final budget and actual statement and the annual receipts and payments account; appointing and working with the examiner/auditor, and following up his or her recommendations; having the accounts formally approved; sending copies to donors and other interested parties; providing other information to donors; preparing the budget and cash-flow forecast for the forthcoming year.

Activities for Chapter 12 *solutions in Appendix C*

12.1 List the financial tasks that should be performed at the following intervals:

Daily

Weekly

Monthly

Annually/at the year-end

Highlight, or add, any tasks:
- that are priorities in the group or organization where you work;
- that are not currently undertaken, but should be. Think about how these tasks could be completed.

CHAPTER 13

Notes for trainers and facilitators, and session plans

The notes in this chapter aim to support trainers and facilitators who wish to use the material in Basic Accounting for Community Organizations and Small Groups *with a group of learners. The notes give some principles for training in basic accounting, a structured programme for a three-day workshop, and suggestions for using the material. It includes a detailed session plan for each of the 12 chapters, showing activities that can be used. Depending on the facilitator's knowledge and experience, variations can be made or additional material added, especially if all the participants are from a single organization.*

Keywords: basic accounting trainer's notes; facilitator's notes on basic accounting for community organizations and small groups; three-day course in basic accounting for community organizations and small groups; facilitating basic accounting workshops; participatory training in basic accounting

The activities and solutions in this book are designed to be used either by someone working on their own, or with a number of people working together with a trainer or facilitator. The activities may form the whole or part of a workshop about basic accounting. The aim is that, after the workshop, participants are able to keep basic accounting records for their own group. These notes are to support someone facilitating this training.

http://dx.doi.org/10.3362/9781780448206.013

Facilitating workshops

Those coming to the workshop will bring different experiences and it is important for the facilitator to recognize this. Some will have already been keeping accounting records, others may not know where to start. The records explained here are enough for a small group to keep their financial affairs in order, but for some it may be just a starting point to learning about more advanced accounting.

Participants will also come with a variety of motives and emotions. Some may be there because they really want to learn the skills. Others may have been forced to attend. Some will be happy to be away from their daily routine, others may be worried that they will look foolish. Accounting may bring back feelings of school mathematics lessons for many, even though in reality it is as much about the techniques used as about numbers. As a facilitator you must work hard to reassure participants that they will succeed in the learning, by being encouraging rather than critical. Above all it is important to make the learning an enjoyable experience.

Most sessions should include an explanation of the purpose of the topic or record being discussed, a demonstration of how to complete it, and time for practice so it becomes familiar. Explain things slowly, asking the participants questions to see how well they have understood, and encourage them to ask you questions too. Be prepared to explain again if necessary. Work on some of the activities in groups of two and three to help people build their confidence, and to allow the more experienced participants to share their knowledge with those who are less experienced.

Participatory approaches

'Participatory training' is when participants are actively involved in their learning, rather than just listening to someone talking. This approach is essential for accounting-based topics where the best way to learn is by having 'hands-on' experience. The material in these activities is designed to allow participants to practise. Ask questions to relate the activities to participants' everyday work in their own organization.

Be aware that people learn in different ways. Try and include a variety of training methods so that it is appropriate for everyone. Use diagrams and visual activities as much as possible to help those who prefer a visual approach, for example, while also encouraging reading, discussing, explaining to others, asking questions, or talking with someone doing similar work.

Invite participants to bring copies of their own group's examples with them, but tell them not to worry if they are not able to do this, or do not understand the terms used – all will be explained at the course! This input helps the course to become more relevant to their needs, as you discuss their material. You can give feedback that participants can take back to their own group. You might ask them to bring an example of their:

- budget;
- budget and actual statement;
- cash and bank book;
- bank statements/pass book;
- receipt voucher;
- receipts and payments account (or equivalent);
- examiner's/auditor's report and recommendations;
- donor proposal and financial reporting formats;
- letter of agreement between a group and a donor.

These can provide additional learning by giving opportunities to identify good practice, and highlight ways in which the records can be developed. Make sure you stress the need for confidentiality with these records, and be careful only to allow constructive criticism. Unless you are working with people from one organization, try to remove the name of the organization before copying any documents.

Structuring the workshop

The material in chapters 1–12 can be used for a workshop. If all the material in this book is used, you would need a workshop of about three days. You may wish to add your own material to provide additional practice, or visits to other organizations which would take extra time.

Start off the workshop and daily sessions with some fun activities to help people relax and feel part of the group. Regularly review the material you have covered with the group, and ask participants to review it for themselves. Use games when participants' energy seems to be dropping. The materials with examples of these activities are listed in the training sections of the Written resources and Web resources at the end of this book.

If you have time you could visit a group locally who already keep good accounting records. Or alternatively ask someone to come from a local group and explain what they do. It is preferable to do this later in the course when most of the material has been covered, and participants know which questions to ask.

A programme for a three-day course is summarized below.

Day	Session	Topic	Learning objective
			At the end of the session participants will be able to:
Day 1 a.m.	1	Introductions and introductory activities (1–1½ hours)	explain why accounts are needed, who should keep the accounts, and the personal qualities of that person.
	2	Deciding what your group's activities will cost (2½–3 hours)	prepare a budget, budget notes and cash-flow forecast and present them in an acceptable format; analyse and raise questions about the information. (Continue if necessary after break.)
Day 1 p.m.		Review main points from morning sessions (15 minutes)	
	3	Records of money coming in and going out (1½–2 hours)	prepare two versions of the cash book, receipts for money received and a table to record cash counted.
	4	Analysing your records to give more information (1–1½ hours)	prepare an analysed cash book for cash transactions.
Day 2 a.m.		Review content of previous day (½ hour)	
	5	Bank accounts (1½–2 hours)	prepare a bank book, a combined cash and bank book, and an analysed cash and bank book.
	6	Making sure that your figures agree with the bank's figures (2½–3 hours)	agree bank book figures with the bank statement/bank pass book, and compile a bank reconciliation statement. (Continue if necessary after break.)

Day	Session	Topic	Learning objective
			At the end of the session participants will be able to:
Day 2 p.m.		Review main points from morning sessions (15 minutes)	
	7	Summarizing the accounts (1 hour)	produce a receipts and payments account and explain what it means.
	8	Summarizing the accounts in more detail (1½–2 hours)	explain the uses and limitations of the receipts and payments account and how to overcome these.
Day 3 a.m.		Review content of previous day (½ hour)	
	9	Providing the information that your group needs (1–1½ hours)	prepare a budget and actual statement from given information, and analyse and raise questions from a statement from an actual group.
	10	Having the accounts checked (1–1½ hours)	discuss what happens when the accounts are checked at the year-end, and explain the value of key documents required for and produced in the process.
Day 3 p.m.	11	Relations with donors (1½–2 hours)	discuss the role of donors, and recognize their financial requirements in relating to budget proposals and reporting.
	12	Regular financial tasks (½–1 hour)	list the regular financial tasks to perform daily, weekly, monthly and yearly.
		End of course (½ hour) (¼ hour) (½ hour)	Action planning and where do you go from here? Course feedback Course summary

Suggestions for using the material

The following session plans are a guide. However, do try and develop the materials in the book further to make them appropriate for the group you are working with. Use participants' own material by asking them to review the documents, identifying their strengths and what could be improved for the future.

The *key points* at the end of each chapter can be used as part of the review process throughout the course. Rather than just showing them, ask participants to identify the key points, maybe at the start or end of each day, to help them remember what you have covered.

Make full use of the *solutions* to help you in guiding the participants as they complete the answer. Many people find their learning is increased by having a copy of the solution, even though they may have reached the same answer on their own. Distribute a copy of each solution – especially for the accounting records activities – for participants to refer to both during and after the course.

The *session plans* make suggestions for working individually, in small groups, or as a whole group. Working with someone else is often helpful to build confidence, particularly in the earlier stages of a course. However, it is also important to prepare some tasks individually, so that you are aware if someone is finding a topic difficult.

It is useful to have some material that you can use when you have a little time to spare. Two suggestions are made in *additional material* at the end of the session plans.

Each session plan shows the figures, activities, solutions, and other documents, that may need to be copied, in **bold**. If everyone has a copy of this book, copies would only be needed of participants' own documents; and donor regulations, proposal forms and reporting templates for Session 11. Some of the materials from this book are available in a 'print ready' format on the Practical Action Publishing website.

Equipment needed

Essential tools include a board or large paper pad and marker pens, to write up ideas for the whole group. Paper copies will be needed of some of the numbered figures in each chapter, and of the activities for participants to complete and their solutions. Calculators are also helpful – ask them to bring their own, if they have one – and a ball is used in one of the activities.

It is useful, although not essential, to have a projector to show some of the outline activities and solutions on a screen. It can help learning if you point to specific parts of a solution in front of the whole group. If not, you can use paper copies.

The aim is that the material can be used anywhere – in a village under a tree, or in a hall with training equipment.

Follow-up

The best courses include some follow-up. The effectiveness of a practical course such as this one is improved if participants feel there is some on-going support, especially for those from smaller groups or organizations who do not have colleagues who know about accounting. Sometimes it is useful for two people to attend from the same group. There are a number of ways of providing follow-up:

- asking participants to write a clear action plan – and then follow up the agreed tasks;
- visiting participants in their place of work to see how they are getting on and to give encouragement;
- establishing a telephone or email help line;
- circulating everyone's contact details so they can support each other;
- encouraging participants to find someone who knows about accounting to act as a mentor – this may be a role for the course facilitator;
- identifying further courses that are appropriate.

Some large donors are willing to fund follow-up activities and these can often be built into a budget proposal. They may include the facilitator (or a member of the donor finance team) visiting regularly to give support, at the same time as others visit to review the programme.

Session plans

Session 1: Introductory activities

Learning objective: at the end of this session participants will be able to explain why accounts are needed, who should keep the accounts, and the personal qualities of that person.
Estimated time: 1–1½ hours

1. If you are using this as the first session of a longer course, ask participants to introduce themselves. If the group is new to each other, ask them to talk with someone else and find out the answers to the following three questions:

- who are you and where were you born?
- what do you do?
- name a mathematics teacher and say what influence they had on you.

Go round the group and ask each person to introduce the person they spoke with.

If the group already know each other ask them to say something about themselves that the others don't know.

2. Say a little about the course programme and anything else they need to know, for example start and finish times, break times, where the toilets are, what happens if there is a fire or other emergency. Ask participants to switch off their phones.

Ask them to think, in groups of three, about their 'expectations' for the course. Get each group to give one or two of their expectations and write them up on a board. Check if there are points here which you need to add to the programme, and say if any are outside the scope of the course.

3. Talk through each of the topics in this session. If the group has no experience of how an organization works, present some of the material in Chapter 1. If they are familiar with this, ask them to think about the questions in the Chapter 1 activities in groups of two (choosing a different partner), and share their own ideas.

4. Use **Activities 1.1 and 1.2** and then allow the groups to feed back. Write up the answers to Activity 1, and then add 'L' or 'I' from the group. Add any items missed from **Solutions 1.1 and 1.2.**

5. Briefly recap what is meant by a 'treasurer'. Use **Activities 1.3 and 1.4** to allow the groups to think further. Ask each group how they got on, and add any missing items from **Solutions 1.3 and 1.4** and discuss any misunderstandings. Answer any questions.

Session 2: Deciding what your group's activities will cost

Learning objective: at the end of this session participants will be able to prepare a budget, budget notes and cash-flow forecast and present them in an acceptable format, and analyse and raise questions about the information.
Estimated time: 2½–3 hours
Advance preparation: ask participants to bring examples of their group's budget.

1. Explain the importance of identifying a group's objectives, as only then can you start to think about what budget items might cost and what money you will need to pay for this. Ask: 'what are the objectives of your group?' Ask: 'how were these objectives agreed?'

2. Explain what is meant by a budget (a list of money we expect to come into and go out of the group). Ask: 'how might you construct a budget from the objectives?' Ask participants if they have had to do this, and how they found/worked out the cost of the items. Show the example of the *Primary Health-care Programme* budget in **Figure 1**. Talk about the layout and headings carefully, explaining how each of the figures might have been calculated. Refer to the notes and other information on page 8, which give a breakdown. Allow plenty of opportunity for questions.

3. Ask participants to list the items (not the values at this stage) of 'money coming in' and 'money going out' that are needed for a small training organization that has recently started to provide courses close to where the participants live. Ask them, in twos, to write down the two lists in **Activity 2.1**. When you have discussed the items people have suggested, ask: 'how would you find how much each of these would cost?'

4. Give out the information about costs in **Activity 2.2**, and the outline sheet on which to write the budget. This activity is best done in groups of two so people feel more confident in preparing the budget. After they have completed it, ask: 'how did you approach the activity?' Distribute **Solution 2.2**, and give them time to look through it and ask questions.

5. Explain that it is good practice to write notes at the end of a budget. These notes show how the calculations have been made. This is useful for anyone looking at the budget, for example a donor, but also for whoever has prepared it so that they can remember what was included. Go through the notes in **Figure 1**. Ask participants to complete the notes for *Training for Development* in **Activity 2.3**. Encourage people to share what they have written.

6. Celebrate with participants that they have prepared a budget – perhaps for the first time! Explain that often budgets are prepared to show to a donor, who may provide funds to help the group achieve their objectives. Ask participants in new pairs to look at each other's budget and notes, imagining in turns that they are someone from a donor organization. Ask them to identify questions, and any information needed, as shown in **Activity 2.4**. Respond to their questions.

Ask: 'how did it feel to be a donor?' and 'can you learn anything from the experience?' Then ask: 'what additional information might the donor ask for?' Answer any outstanding questions.

7. Explain why it is helpful to break down a budget month by month. This will help us to see *when* the money will be received and paid. It will also help to assess whether the money is actually received and paid in the pattern we think it will be. Explain that breaking down the budget over months is a forecast for the future. It may be possible to rearrange the pattern of money coming in or going out, if it is shown for example that more is going out than coming in, in a particular month. Say that this table is sometimes called a 'cash-flow forecast'.

Show the *Primary Health-care Programme* example in **Figures 2a, 2b and 3**. Be careful to explain Figure 3 showing the calculations adding 'money coming in' to the amount at the start of the month, then taking away from this 'money going out'. This then calculates the estimated amount remaining at the end of the month. Explain how the figure at the end of one month becomes the starting point for the following month.

Refer to the month of June where the closing figure is shown in brackets, explaining that it shows the figure is expected to be negative, unless we change the pattern of money coming in and/or going out. Ask: 'are there any items that could be received earlier or paid later to avoid this negative figure in June?' Think through the consequences of what they suggest, and answer any questions.

8. When participants feel happy with this approach introduce **Activity 2.5**. Say we will use the details about *Training for Development's* budget, and when money will come in and go out. We are going to prepare a similar table, and the first three months have already been completed as a guide. Talk through what is required and prepare April together. Then ask the group to complete the rest of the table. Make sure calculators are available if needed. Help participants and check their figures for 'money coming in' and 'money going out' to make sure these are correct before they start to summarize the calculations in the bottom section of the table.

As individuals finish, ask: 'what could be changed to avoid the estimated negative balances at the end of certain months?' When most have finished, distribute **Solution 2.5** and compare the different figures calculated. Say that the figures will depend on assumptions you have made. Then go to **Activity 2.6** and write up problems and possible solutions.

Introduce **Activity 2.7** by asking what a donor might say when they see the cash-flow forecast. Provide feedback, and answer any remaining questions.

9. If participants have access to a computer suggest they enter **Solution 2.5** into a spreadsheet. A downloadable version of a 'programmed' cash-flow forecast spreadsheet, in a similar format to the one in the solution, is shown at: www.johncammack. net (click on 'resources' and 'project budgeting').

10. If participants are able to bring copies of their own group's budgets, ask them to look through them, identifying the strengths and what could be improved. Ask for feedback from the groups. Encourage them to say what they liked, and what could be improved.

Session 3: Records of money coming in and going out

Learning objective: at the end of this session participants will be able to prepare two versions of the cash book, receipts for money received, and a table to record cash counted.
Estimated time: 1½–2 hours
Advance preparation: ask participants to bring an example of their group's receipts that are issued when money is received.

1. Ask: 'what are the most important rules in keeping accounts?' Responses may include:

- the accounts are accurate;
- the accounts are up to date;
- someone is responsible;
- it is well organized.

Allow everyone to respond before giving the answer. Say all these points are important, but the two most important are:

- make sure everything is written down;
- keep every piece of paper.

Write up these two 'golden' rules, and display them throughout the rest of the course.

Explain that this session will show how to write everything down, so that the 'money coming in' and the 'money going out', is in an acceptable format. This format is often referred to as the 'cash book'. It will also look at some of the pieces of paper that need to be kept.

2. Show the layout of the cash book in **Figure 6**. Go through the items one by one, explain how the balance is calculated, and answer any questions. Then show the information in **Activity 3.1**, asking participants to complete the cash book and calculate the balance after each transaction. Give out copies of **Solution 3.1** and make sure everyone has the correct final balance.

3. Explain the importance of receipts and show the examples in **Activity 3.2**. Ask participants to complete the remaining receipts and then include the receipt numbers in the spare column of the outline of Activity 3.1. Provide feedback and answer any questions. If possible, look at an example of participants' own receipts, and their differing format. Ask participants to identify what they like about them and how they could be improved. Ask: 'why is it important to pre-number receipts?' (answer: to make sure receipts are not lost, or stolen and then issued, without someone noticing).

4. Say that there are different ways of completing the cash book, and why it is helpful to include more information than that in Activity 3.1. Show the cash book layout in **Figure 9**, and say that this is completed using the information that we have already used for Activities 3.1 and 3.2. Explain each of the items, the additional columns, and the significance of the closing balance. Ask participants to complete **Activity 3.3.**

Answer any questions and provide feedback. Say that this way of presenting the cash book will be useful as we develop it in the next session.

5. Ask each participant to write down five rules to help control the cash that a group holds. Give an example of: 'it is important for the person responsible for the cash to count it regularly'. Gather their suggestions and go through the **rules to help you to control your cash** (Chapter 3).

6. Refer back to the rules about counting cash and say we will look at a way of recording what cash a group has. Introduce the activity and ask participants to complete the table in **Activity 3.4**. Answer questions, provide feedback and distribute **Solution 3.4**.

7. Let participants complete the multiple choice questions in **Activity 3.5** and give feedback on the suggestions. This will summarize some of the rules about controlling cash. Answer any remaining questions.

Session 4: Analysing your records to give more information

Learning objective: at the end of this session participants will be able to prepare an analysed cash book for cash transactions. **Estimated time:** 1–1½ hours

1. Review **Activity 3.3** and ask 'what does the cash book tell us?' Ask 'what information does the cash book not tell us?' Draw out answers including:

- it does not show how the money has been spent against the budget;
- we do not know how much has been spent on each category of receipt or payment.

2. Explain that we sometimes need the cash book to show us the amounts received and paid according to what we have planned in the budget. Show the example of an analysed cash book in **Figure 15**. Talk through the outline and explain how the totalled items for each analysed column add up to the total 'cash amount' column. Ask participants to complete **Activity 4.2**. Distribute **Solution 4.2**. Answer questions and provide feedback.

3. If participants have access to a computer, suggest they complete **Activity 4.3**, by putting **Solution 4.2** into a spreadsheet program. If participants are new to spreadsheets, this may be an opportunity to learn how to include basic formulae, for example to total the columns. If participants have used the downloadable spreadsheet in Session 2 (paragraph 9), with the formulae already included, this is a logical next step.

4. Summarize the session by completing the sentences in **Activity 4.1** and give feedback.

Session 5: Bank accounts

Learning objective: at the end of this session participants will be able to prepare a bank book, a combined cash and bank book, and an analysed cash and bank book.
Estimated time: 1½–2 hours
Advance preparation: ask participants to bring an example of their cash and bank book, and if possible, an analysed cash and bank book.

1. Start by asking what participants know already about bank accounts. Write up ideas. Explain the different types that are offered, and how we record bank account transactions using the bank book. Ask: 'what bank accounts does your group have?'

2. Show and talk through the example in **Figure 18**. Say this is similar to the cash book that we have already completed. Ask participants to complete the bank book in **Activity 5.2**. Answer questions and provide feedback about the activity. Distribute **Solution 5.2**.

3. Explain that you can keep the cash book and bank book separately, but sometimes it is helpful and easier to show the two records together on one page in date order. Explain this further by talking through **Figure 21**.

Ask participants to prepare an example of this for *Training for Development* in **Activity 5.3**. Make sure copies of the details from **Activities 3.1 and 5.2** are available. Provide feedback and answer questions about the activity.

4. Ask: 'when would it be appropriate to use this presentation?' and 'how could it be useful?' Then ask 'what additional information would be helpful to support this cash and bank book?' Say that the analysed cash and bank book would provide even more information, and say that we will look at an example later.

5. Ask: 'what do we need to remember when filling in our bank book record?' Write up the points identified and then compare with the 'points to remember when filling in your bank book' in Chapter 5. Answer any questions about these points.

6. Go back to the 'analysed cash and bank book' and show the outlines in **Activity 5.4**. Ask the participants to complete the outlines. Make sure the information in Activities 3.1 and 5.2 is available. Answer any questions and provide feedback. Distribute **Solution 5.4**.

Talk through what happens when money is moved between the cash and bank accounts. Show the examples in **Figures 19 and 20**, and answer any questions. Ask participants to complete **Activity 5.5** in twos. Show the completed solution and answer any questions. Distribute **Solution 5.5**.

7. To summarize the work on bank accounts, ask participants to complete the three sections in **Activity 5.1** in small groups. Give feedback.

8. If anyone has brought copies of their group's accounting records for cash and bank combined and/or analysed cash and bank records, allow them to show these to other participants. Encourage comments on the way they are presented and possible improvements.

Session 6: Making sure that your figures agree with the bank's figures

Learning objective: at the end of this session participants will be able to agree a bank book's figures with the bank statement/bank pass book, and compile a bank reconciliation statement.
Estimated time: 2½–3 hours
Advance preparation: ask participants to bring examples of their group's bank statement/pass book, and cash/bank books for the same period. Alternatively, if all the participants are from one group or organization, you may like to copy some actual examples for everyone.

Participants may find this session more technically challenging, so allow time to go through it in detail. When they have completed the Chapter 6 activities, try to find a real example to use for additional practice. Make use of the bank reconciliation statement outline in Appendix B, **Figure 51**.

1. Ask: 'why might a group's bank book record be different from the bank statement/pass book?' Expect answers such as:

- cheques have been issued at the month-end, but not yet presented to the bank or shown on the statement;
- money has been paid in to the bank at the month-end and not yet included in the statement;
- bank charges or interest appear on the statement, but have not yet been recorded in the bank book;
- bank transfers on the statement are not yet recorded in the bank book.

If participants are likely to have their own bank account, you could draw out the similarities to this. Say: 'for our own bank account we can probably remember what we have received and paid, but a group is likely to have more transactions and it needs a formal way to remember the differences.'

2. Talk through **Figure 26**. Go through this carefully, particularly the two columns explaining the purpose of the sub-totals. Show how the totals are added to/subtracted from each other and why. Then look at the example of the bank book and bank statement for the *Primary Health-care Programme* in **Figure 27a.** Identify the four stages of preparing a bank reconciliation statement:

- Enter any outstanding items in your bank book to bring it up to date.
- Include any charges or interest from the bank statement in your bank book.
- Tick off the items that appear in your bank book *and* in the bank's records.
- Construct a table to show how the two records agree. Include all items that are not ticked off.

3. Go through each of these four stages in turn, and show the adjustments in **Figure 27b.** Then show how the bank reconciliation statement is produced and show **Figure 28.** Make sure the bullet points in the 'comments on the reconciliation' in Chapter 6 are all mentioned in the discussion. Answer any questions.

4. Ask participants to complete the similar example for *Training for Development* in **Activity 6.2,** using the four stages (shown in paragraph 2 above). Support them to complete the bank reconciliation statement. As participants finish the task, ask them to start on **Activity 6.3.** When everyone has finished the bank reconciliation, distribute and talk through **Solution 6.2.** Ask the whole group: 'what actions would you take after preparing the bank reconciliation statement?' Make sure the two points in **Solution 6.3** are highlighted. Give feedback and answer any questions.

5. Explain that some bank reconciliation statements can include cheques from previous months which have still not appeared on the bank statement. If this happens, the month's opening balances in the bank book and on the bank statement are not the same. The first task is to reconcile the opening balance. In a real situation you may simply be able to look at the previous month's bank reconciliation statement to see why there is a difference.

Ask participants to attempt **Activity 6.4.** Start by showing **Figure 32a**, and explain the effect of the two cheques outstanding at 30 April. Support participants as they complete the 'four stages' and prepare the bank reconciliation statement in **Figure 32b**. As participants finish, ask them to raise questions about the statement as in **Activity 6.5.**

When everyone has finished, distribute **Solution 6.4** and check participants have calculated it correctly and understand the answer. Ask: 'what questions should be raised about the statement?' and make sure all the questions in **Solution 6.5** are included. Give further feedback and answer any questions.

6. Ask the participants to work in groups of three to think up some rules to control your bank account. Allow 5–10 minutes. Write up the responses. Compare with the **rules to help you to control your bank account** in Chapter 6.

7. Use **Activities 6.1 and 6.6** for participants to review their own learning. Ask them to complete these individually. Go round the group and ask them to say what they have written. Allow everyone to contribute.

8. If you have **a real example of a bank book and bank statement**, use this for additional practice of bank reconciliations.

Session 7: Summarizing the accounts

Learning objective: at the end of this session participants will be able to produce a receipts and payments account and explain what it means.
Estimated time: 1 hour

1. Introduce the topic by explaining that at the end of a month/year, we need to produce a summary of our financial transactions for a group's internal use, and to distribute to donors, service users, government, and anyone else who is interested.

Explain that there are various types of end-of-year accounting statement that can be produced, but that the one we will prepare is a straightforward way of summarizing the money coming in and money going out – it is called a 'receipts and payments account'.

2. Explain that sometimes the receipts and payments account is produced at the end of each month and we will consider how it might look for the *Primary Health-care Programme*. Use the analysed cash and bank book as the basis of the information we prepare. Look first at the receipts side and show **Figure 34.** Go through the items, and introduce the idea and show an example of breaking down a figure, for example grants, to give more information. Ask participants to complete the receipts side of a receipts and payments account for *Training for Development* in **Activity 7.1.** Provide feedback.

3. Show **Figure 35** and explain how we exclude cash to bank and bank to cash transfers in the receipts and payments account.

4. Talk through the payment example in **Figure 36.** Ask participants to complete **Activity 7.2** and provide any feedback.

5. Ask participants to put this all together in **Activity 7.3.** Remind them to add the name of the group or organization, the title, and the period covered by the account. Give feedback when completed and distribute **Solution 7.3.** Answer any further questions.

Session 8: Summarizing the accounts with more information

Learning objective: at the end of this session participants will be able to explain the uses and limitations of the receipts and payments account and how to overcome the limitations.
Estimated time: 1½–2 hours
Advance preparation: Ask participants to bring a copy of their group's end-of-year receipts and payments account (or its equivalent).

This session aims to show the uses and limitations of the receipts and payments account, and to examine how notes can be added to the account to provide additional information.

1. Ask: 'what does the receipts and payments account show?'
Expect responses including:

- how much money (cash and bank) is left at the end of the period;
- how much the group has received and paid over the period;
- the amounts received and paid against budget items (for this we would need to compare the account with the budget).

Say these are useful points to highlight. Stress a major benefit is that the account is straightforward to prepare.

2. Then ask: 'what does the receipts and payments account not show – what are its limitations?' Expect responses such as:

- The items in the receipts and payments account are not all for the same period of time. Amounts are sometimes paid in advance, or owed by the group at the end of the accounting period.
- Long-term items, such as office equipment, are treated the same as short-term items. For example, office equipment may last for several years, whereas rent is only for this period.
- The cash and bank balance does not show a surplus (profit) or deficit (loss). It is therefore difficult to see how the group is performing financially, other than whether there is money available in cash and at the bank.

Give help to the group to identify these items if they need it. Say these points mean that although the account is a useful summary of receipts, payments and the cash and bank balance, it has limitations.

3. Explain that we can add notes to the receipts and payments account. Ask them to use the three limitations above in paragraph 2, and think of ways to overcome these as in **Activity 8.1**. Allow 10 minutes for this; then write up the ideas from the group. Use **Solution 8.1** to help identify the ways of overcoming the limitations.

4. Look at each limitation in turn, and show an example of how these might look, such as:

- The record of outstanding items at the end of the year should be prepared. For example, grants may be received for two years in advance, but rent may only have been paid for 10 months by the end of the year. Ask the participants to write any notes that might appear at the bottom on the *Training for Development* receipts and payments account in **Solution 7.3**. Participants can make assumptions about what might have happened. Give feedback on their notes.
- Show the note in **Figure 43** that lists fixed assets bought during the year for the *Primary Health-care Programme*. Explain how this might distort the cash/bank figure at the end of the account: for example, if a vehicle that would last for several years was bought and shown as a payment in just one year.
- The balance shows only the cash and bank amount at the end of the accounting period. To provide a surplus or deficit, a different accounting statement would be needed.

Although this is not possible with the receipts and payments account, the notes help to describe the reasoning for these limitations, and the effect it has on the final cash/bank figure.

5. Go through the section on 'Saving money to replace items that will wear out' in Chapter 8. Explain the reasons why a group may save money in this way. Ask participants to complete **Activity 8.2**, or talk about the reasons at the start of the following session/day to review these ideas.

6. Show the example of a receipts and payments account for a whole year in **Appendix A**. Allow time for participants to look through the example. Divide them into groups of three, and ask each group to identify questions they might ask the *Waterside Community Centre* if they were the donor providing the 'development grant' or some of the 'donations'. Ask them to write their questions on a large piece of paper. Compare the different questions. Provide feedback and mention any additional questions they could ask. Ask: 'what additional information would be useful to compare with this receipts and payments account?'

Expect responses such as:

- the same year's budget;
- the comparative receipts and payments account figures for the previous year;
- the following year's budget.

7. Show an example of a **real receipts and payments account**, if possible, from one of their own groups. Divide into groups of three, to identify the account's strengths and what could be improved in the presentation for the following year. Provide feedback, and allow time for any further questions. Make sure that any negative comments are stated as constructive feedback if you are using their own accounts. If necessary, stress the need for confidentiality.

8. End the session by saying that the receipts and payments account will produce a summarized statement at the end of the accounting period. However, when a group starts to grow (for example, when it has more employees, or owns vehicles and equipment), it will need to produce a more complex financial summary. Such accounts are outside the scope of this course, but tell them if you know about other relevant courses.

Session 9: Providing the information that your group needs

Learning objective: at the end of this session participants will be able to prepare a budget and actual statement from given information, and analyse and raise questions about a statement from an actual group.
Estimated time: 1–1½ hours
Advance preparation: Ask participants to bring a real example of a 'budget and actual statement'.

1. Explain that the receipts and payments account is a useful document and, although it can be produced monthly, it is usually prepared at the end of a financial year. We often need a document to see what we have received and paid so far, compared with the budgeted amounts. This helps us to identify whether the group is progressing financially as we expected when we prepared the budget.

2. Present **Figure 44** and explain the columns and what they show. Go through each of the notes and the 'what does the statement show?' section in Chapter 9. Explain the importance of asking questions when you interpret such a statement.

3. Ask participants to complete the budget and actual statement for *Training for Development* in **Activity 9.1**. As they finish ask them to think about **Activity 9.2**. Distribute **Solution 9.1** and compare the figures. Discuss the reasons from **Activity 9.2**. Give feedback.

4. Ask: 'why might *Training for Development* not have made an entry for transfer to a savings account?' as in **Activity 9.3**. Then ask: 'if it had been included, where would it have appeared?'

5. Talk about the importance of notes with a budget and actual statement. Ask them to complete **Activity 9.4**. Distribute **Solution 9.4** and give any feedback.

6. Explain that, as the year progresses, a group needs not only to compare the budget with actual receipts and payments for the current month, but also for all the months of the financial year to date. Show how this can presented in **Figure 45**. If possible use a **budget and actual statement example**, covering several months, from one of the participants' own groups. If not, find a real example from a group you know. Ask them to imagine they were the leaders of that group, and list the questions they would ask. Give feedback. Ask: 'what do you like about the presentation?' and 'is there anything that could be improved?'

Session 10: Having the accounts checked

Learning objective: at the end of this session participants will be able to discuss what happens when the accounts are checked at the year-end, and explain the value of key documents required for and produced in the process.
Estimated time: 1–1½ hours

Advance preparation: Ask participants to bring with them copies of 'independent examiner/audit reports' or '(independent) examiner/audit recommendations' (also called a 'management letter').

1. Ask: 'why is it important that someone, other than the person keeping the accounts, reviews them at least once a year?' Expect responses such as:

- to show that the person keeping the accounts is honest;
- to find any mistakes;
- to let the group's leaders, donors and others know that the accounts are in good order;
- to allow someone else to give valuable advice about accounting.

Stress that people who give money will only be happy to do this if someone independent of the group can guarantee yearly that the accounting is in good order. Say that the person who reviews the account is called either an 'examiner' or an 'auditor'.

Explain that these terms vary internationally, but generally an examiner (or independent examiner) can be a 'lighter touch' audit for a small organization. You might like to add something about the legal requirements for audit in your own country. Ask: 'what do you think is the most important quality of an examiner/auditor?' (answer: independence). Ask: 'why is this?' Give the answer if necessary, and say why independence is important for objectivity.

2. Say that the examination/audit usually takes place after the end of the financial year. Although the level of checking varies, there are certain records that an examiner or auditor may wish to see – **Activity 10.2**. Ask participants what these could be, and write up a list. The records are shown in **Solution 10.2**. Mention any records that the group has missed.

3. If possible, show some examples of documents produced by an examiner or auditor from one of the participants. These might include an:

- examiner's/auditor's recommendations/management letter;
- examiner's/auditor's report.

If not, try and find an example from a local organization. Ask participants to spend some time in groups of two or three, finding what these documents actually say or are asking the group to do. Explain that sometimes they are written with standard audit phrases that are not always easy to understand. Give feedback as necessary.

4. Ask: 'what are the consequences of not having your accounts examined or audited?' – **Activity 10.4.** Possible responses are shown in **Solution 10.4.**

5. Say that auditors from organizations who give your group money may also want to look at your accounts. It is good practice to welcome them. Ask: 'has anyone had experience of examinations/audits?' Draw out their experience and allow the group to discuss.

Session 11: Relations with donors

Learning objective: at the end of this session participants will be able to discuss the role of donors, and recognize their financial requirements in relating to budget proposals and reporting.
Estimated time: 1½–2 hours
Advance preparation: Ask participants to bring with them an example of a funding proposal, donor financial report, and a letter of agreement between their group and a donor.
Find an example of donor regulations, a budget proposal, a financial reporting template, and a letter of agreement from a donor likely to fund the groups represented. If you are able to find versions from several donors, even better!

1. Say that many groups rely of outside funding to keep them going. These funding sources are referred to as donors. Ask: 'can you think of organizations who give community groups/ organizations money to help fund their activities?' See list in the section 'Who are the donors?' in Chapter 11.
Explain that some of the bigger donors provide money to international or national organizations, who then pass it on

to community groups. It is important for organizations that pass money from international/national donors to be able to account fully. They will expect community groups to report to them so they can pass this accounting on to their donors.

2. Ask: 'what experience do you have of working with a donor?' Lead a discussion about their experience and the funding role of donors. Give everyone a chance to contribute.

3. Follow the discussion by looking at an example of regulations from a donor. Ask participants to look through it, to circle any regulations that surprise them, and highlight any where they are not sure what it means. Allow everyone to say what surprised them and discuss the reasons why this might be required. Then answer any clarification questions raised by participants.

4. Obtain a **budget proposal** from a donor (this can often be downloaded from donor websites). Make a copy for each participant and go through it in detail, thinking through how they might approach the task of filling it in. Ask participants to complete it with the details from **Solutions 2.2 and 2.3** for *Training for Development*. Provide feedback and answer any questions.

As part of the follow-up discussion ask for answers to the donor's questions listed in **Solution 2.4**. Ask: 'how might you respond to these questions?'

5. Obtain a donor financial reporting template. Make a copy for everyone and go through it, thinking through how they might approach completing it. Ask them to fill it in with the details from **Solution 9.1 and 9.4** for *Training for Development*. Provide feedback and answer any questions.

Ask: 'what information could you provide to avoid the questions asked by the donor in **Solution 9.5**?' Give feedback.

6. Explain what happens for those responsible for accounting when a group receives significant extra funding. Show an example of a **letter of agreement** between a group and a donor. Say that these are useful documents to make sure both partners know what is expected of each other. Explain what donors require when they provide funding for tendering and purchasing of goods and services.

Use **Activities 11.1 and 11.2** as a way of consolidating the session. Go through the answers.

Session 12: Regular financial tasks

Learning objective: at the end of this session participants will be able to list the regular financial tasks to perform daily, weekly, monthly and yearly.
Estimated time: ½–1 hour

1. Copy the **daily, weekly, monthly and yearly financial tasks** in Chapter 12. Allow participants time to read through them, one by one. Then go through the tasks and answer any questions. Do this for all four documents, one by one. It may be useful for participants to think this through with someone else.

2. As you complete each period, ask: 'are there any other tasks that you would need to complete?' Ask them to add them to the list, then to cross off anything that is not relevant for their group. Each time ask them to tell you what they have added and deleted. Make sure items are not deleted just because someone does not really understand them. Ask: 'are there any tasks listed here that you don't currently do?' and 'which tasks listed are the most important?'

End of course

Action planning and 'where do you go from here' *(½ hour).* It is important, at the end of the course, to allow time for participants to identify what they want to take away from the course, and to commit themselves to it. This helps the transition back to their group after the course ends. This planning has been started in session 12, but it is important to allow some 'action planning' time to give them a chance to think more broadly.

Give participants a piece of paper and ask them to write down three ideas that they want to take away with them.

To add to their commitment ask them to say, in front of the group, one (or more) of their ideas. Ask them to answer the question: 'where do you go from here in learning about basic accounting?' Encourage their plans, but you often need to make no other comments. Leave them to do most of the talking. Tell them if there is any follow-up to this course (for example visits, email/telephone support, future courses).

Course feedback *(¼ hour)*. It is helpful for you and the participants to see/hear feedback about the course. It's a really good way for everyone to learn from the experience and to build this into improvements for future courses. You may want to use a **questionnaire** asking what participants thought about the course, and ask for verbal comments.

Course summary *(½ hour or less)*. This can take as long as you have, and it is good to finish the course with a summary of what you have covered. A fun way to do this is ask the group to tell a story which must include something that you have talked about in your time together. Use a soft **ball**, or anything soft to throw around, start the story yourself with '... once upon a time there was someone who kept the accounts for a group ...' and then throw the ball to someone else to continue the story. When they have contributed, they pass the ball to someone else. Make sure everyone has had a go before the ball returns to you. Then say '... then after a really busy time, they went home and lived happily ever after'.

Additional material

Terminology quiz (½ hour or as long as available). This can be used whenever you have a some spare time. It helps to consolidate the material. Simply write up a number of terms – one for each person and a few extra ones – from the Glossary at the beginning of this book. These should be ones that you have already used in the course.

Go round the participants and ask them to choose a term, and give a definition. It becomes increasingly difficult as you go round the group as there are fewer terms to choose from. Give positive feedback and gently correct any misunderstandings.

Further questions (*½ hour or as long as available*). Do this at the end of a session/day or when you have some spare time. Ask participants, in groups of two, to think of/write down one question they still have unanswered, relating to the material you have covered so far. Doing this in twos means participants are more confident in asking a question to which they may suspect others already know the answer. Ask the group when it comes back together to help you to provide the answers. Carry on as long as you need to.

Appendices

The appendices include an additional example of a receipts and payments account, blank accounting templates, and full solutions to the activities at the end of each chapter. In addition there are details of written and web resources that may be useful.

Keywords: receipts and payments account example; blank forms for basic accounting; solutions to activities in *Basic Accounting for Community Organizations and Small Groups*; written resources for non-profit basic accounting; web resources for non-profit basic accounting

http://dx.doi.org/10.3362/9781780448206.013

APPENDIX A

Example of a receipts and payments account
(with added notes and comparative figures for the previous year)

Waterside Community Centre

Annual Receipts and Payments Account for the period 1 April 20-- to 31 March 20--

Last year's amount		Note	Amount	Total amount
	Receipts			
3,687	Opening balance,1 April 20--			**8,946**
–	Development grant	1	6,000	
31,329	Donations	2	31,365	
25,468	Fees	3	34,751	
56,797	**Total receipts**			**72,116**
60,484				**81,062**
	Payments			
–	Purchase of equipment	4	6,155	
–	Transfer to savings account	5	1,862	
33,125	Salaries		40,028	
6,205	Materials		8,759	
3,520	Travel costs		3,812	
5,933	Rent of centre	6	7,780	
902	Electricity	7	861	
296	Water charge	6	396	
	Office costs			
450	telephone	8	572	
1,045	printing, postage, stationery		959	
62	bank charges		104	
51,538	**Total payments**			**71,288**
8,946	**Balance, 31 March 20--**	9		**9,774**

Notes to the account

1 The **development grant** was given by the Education Department for the purchase of new equipment (see also note 4).

2 **Donations** received from:

	Amount
Development Trust	5,000
Co-operative Skills Association	11,365
Rural Assistance Fund	15,000
Total	**31,365**

3 **Fees** include 810.00 paid in advance for June 20--.

4 **Purchase of fixed assets** (equipment):

	Cost
Projector and screen	4,257
Audio equipment	1,898
Total	**6,155**

5 **Amount transferred to savings account** is for the eventual replacement of the projector and screen and audio equipment.

6 **Rent of centre and water charges** cover the period 1 April 20-- to 31 March 20--.

7 **Electricity** paid is for 11 months (April to February). It is estimated that the March charge will be 75.00, payable in June.

8 **Telephone** payment includes 35.00 for two months' rental in advance.

9 **Breakdown of cash/bank amounts** held at 31 March 20--:

	Amount	Total amount
Balance in cash, 31 March		648
Balance in current account, 31 March		3,756
Balance in deposit account, 31 March		5,370
Total of cash, current, and deposit account		**9,774**
Balance in savings account, 31 March:		
replacement of projector and screen	1,288	
replacement of audio equipment	574	1,862
Total		**11,636**

APPENDIX B

Some blank forms which you may find useful

Figure 47 A cash-flow forecast format

PERIOD																		TOTAL
MONEY COMING IN																		
Total [A]																		
MONEY GOING OUT																		
Total [B]																		
Money at start of month [C]																		
Plus total money coming in [A]																		
Less total money going out [B]																		
Money at end of month [C+A–B]																		

Figure 48 An analysed cash and bank book format (receipts side)

Date	Details	Receipt number	Cash amount	Bank amount							
	Opening balance										
	Totals										

Figure 49 An analysed cash and bank book format (payments side)

Date	Details	Payment number	Cheque number	Cash amount	Bank amount									
	Totals													

Closing balance ....

Figure 50 A cash-count format

Cash counted as at	Value	multiplied by	Number	equals	Total value
Notes:		×		=	
		×		=	
		×		=	
		×		=	
		×		=	
Coins:		×		=	
		×		=	
		×		=	
		×		=	
		×		=	
Total cash counted					....
Cash book balance at					.
Difference* (if any)					....

*Action to be taken regarding any difference:

Counted by .... Date .... Agreed by .... Date ....

Figure 51 A bank reconciliation statement format

BANK RECONCILIATION STATEMENT AS AT			
	Amount	Total amount	
Bank balance at .... (from bank statement)		....	[A]
Less: cheques not yet included in the bank's records			
cheque number	....		
cheque number	....		
cheque number	....	....	[B: total cheques]
	Sub-total		[A–B]
Plus: items paid in but not yet included in the bank's records			
paying-in reference	....		
paying-in reference	....	....	[C]
Balance in bank book at .... (group's own record)		....	[A–B+C]

[The letters A, B, and C are included to show where calculations are made.]

APPENDIX C

Solutions to activities in Chapters 1–12

1 Introduction: why keep accounts – and who should keep them?

1.1
Answers should include the following:

a. Members of the group need to know what money is available, and how it has been spent. (I)
b. Accounting is often required by law. (L)
c. Donors require a report on their funds. (L)
d. The information is valuable in running the group. (I)
e. It shows that the person who looks after the money is honest. (I)

1.2
See above. Although some accounting is required by law or an outside organization, one of the main purposes is to help the group to achieve its objectives.

1.3
Answers should include:

a. Honesty.
b. A methodical approach.
c. Ability to keep accurate records.
d. Confidence in dealing with money.
e. Confidence in communicating with employees of a bank and other organizations.
f. Ability to explain money matters to those who have less experience.

1.4
Answers should include:

a. Help the group to plan objectives (M); to keep accurate accounting records (M); to prepare summaries of how money has been spent (H); to arrange for an independent person to check the accounts once a year (L); to communicate with the bank (M); to arrange payment of salaries and bills (M).

b. See above, for suggestions of 'high' (H), 'medium' (M), and 'low' (L). If the treasurer does not have skills to complete all the high-level tasks (for example, summarizing the accounts at the year-end), it may be possible to pay someone, possibly an accountant, who has these skills to complete this task.

c. All of the group, or the management committee on their behalf, and the staff, if any, need to be concerned to make sure there is sound financial management. This will be demanded by those who give you money and will help to make the most of the resources available to achieve your objectives.

2 Deciding what your group's activities will cost

2.1
Possible answers:

Money coming in
grants
fees for training
sale of materials

Money going out
salaries
office expenses
> for example: electricity, water, travel, accommodation
> training venue, equipment, audit fee
training equipment

2.2

Money coming in

Item	Amount
Department of Education 'start-up' grant	25,000
Grant 1	30,000
Grant 2	40,000
Fees for training	66,000
Sale of materials	1,200
Total of 'money coming in'	**162,200**

Money going out

Item	Amount
Co-ordinator's salary	12,000
Administrator's salary	9,000
Part-time trainers	24,000
Office rent	12,000
Electricity, water, telephone	17,000
Training materials	6,000
Office expenses (including audit fee)	14,000
Travel and accommodation	18,000
Hire of training rooms	21,000
Office equipment	13,000
Training equipment	11,000
Total of 'money going out'	**157,000**
Difference	**5,200**

2.3
Notes
(If additional information were available, these notes could include more detail.)

1 Funding is confirmed for all grants.
2 Fees for training, based on 10 courses per month, producing 550.00 each.

3 Sale of materials, based on sales worth 100.00 per month.
4 Co-ordinator's salary at 12,000.00 per year includes employer's taxes.
5 Administrator's salary at 9,000.00 per year includes employer's taxes.
6 Part-time trainers: four at 6,000.00 per year, including employer's taxes.
7 Fixed contract for one year's rent.
8 Annual electricity charge of 7,000.00, plus combined water and telephone costs of 10,000.00.
9 Training materials: 10 courses per month at 50.00 per course.
10 Office expenses: audit fee of 5,000.00, plus other costs at 750.00 per month.
11 Travel and accommodation costs, based on five people at 300.00 each per month.
12 Hire of training rooms – needed for five courses per month at 350.00 each. Other accommodation provided by trainees' own organizations.
13 Office equipment: four desks at 500.00; seven chairs at 250.00; filing cabinet at 700.00; additional furniture for offices 8,550.00.
14 Training equipment: projector and screen 4,800.00; television 3,000.00; audio equipment 3,200.00.

2.4
A donor's questions might include the following:

- What is the basis for the estimates?
- Are the estimated training fees realistic?
- For how long are the donors committed to the project?
- When will the money be received?
- Are the salaries similar to other organizations?
- Will the 1,000.00 not needed for start-up equipment be returned? (25,000.00 grant *less* 24,000.00, planned spending on equipment)
- What is the 'additional furniture'?

Information to be provided:

- A breakdown of the calculations for each budget item. (The notes in Activity 2.3 provide this.)
- Further notes added to the budget to justify any unusual items.
- A cash-flow forecast, to predict when money will be received and paid.
- Written estimates from suppliers for the cost of office and training equipment, if available.

2.5

Figure 52 *Training for Development* cash-flow forecast for 1 January to 31 December

	JAN	FEB	MAR	APR	MAY	JUN	JUL	AUG	SEP	OCT	NOV	DEC	TOTAL
MONEY COMING IN													
DOE 'start-up' grant	25,000												25,000
Grant - donor 1	15,000				15,000								30,000
Grant - donor 2						40,000							40,000
Fees for training	5,500	5,500	5,500	5,500	5,500	5,500	5,500	5,500	5,500	5,500	5,500	5,500	66,000
Sale of materials	100	100	100	100	100	100	100	100	100	100	100	100	1,200
Total [A]	45,600	5,600	5,600	5,600	20,600	45,600	5,600	5,600	5,600	5,600	5,600	5,600	162,200
MONEY GOING OUT													
Co-ordinator's salary	1,000	1,000	1,000	1,000	1,000	1,000	1,000	1,000	1,000	1,000	1,000	1,000	12,000
Administrator's salary	750	750	750	750	750	750	750	750	750	750	750	750	9,000
Trainer's salaries	2,000	2,000	2,000	2,000	2,000	2,000	2,000	2,000	2,000	2,000	2,000	2,000	24,000
Office rent	6,000					6,000							12,000
Electricity,water,telephone	7,000		2,500			2,500			2,500			2,500	17,000
Training materials	500	500	500	500	500	500	500	500	500	500	500	500	6,000
Office expenses (including audit)	750	750	750	750	750	750	750	750	750	750	750	750	14,000
Travel/accommodation	1,500	1,500	1,500	1,500	1,500	1,500	1,500	1,500	1,500	1,500	1,500	1,500	18,000
Hire of training rooms	1,750	1,750	1,750	1,750	1,750	1,750	1,750	1,750	1,750	1,750	1,750	1,750	21,000
Office equipment	13,000												13,000
Training equipment	11,000												11,000
Total [B]	45,250	8,250	10,750	8,250	8,250	16,750	8,250	8,250	10,750	8,250	8,250	15,750	157,000
Money at start of month [C]	0	350	(2,300)	(7,450)	(10,100)	2,250	31,100	28,450	25,800	20,650	18,000	15,350	
Plus total money coming in [A]	45,600	5,600	5,600	5,600	20,600	45,600	5,600	5,600	5,600	5,600	5,600	5,600	
Less total money going out [B]	45,250	8,250	10,750	8,250	8,250	16,750	8,250	8,250	10,750	8,250	8,250	15,750	
Money at end of month [C+A–B]	350	(2,300)	(7,450)	(10,100)	2,250	31,100	28,450	25,800	20,650	18,000	15,350	5,200	

2.6
Problems

- Overdrawn position in February, March, and April.
- Large amounts of money in hand later in the year.

Solutions

- Contact the donors, show them the cash-flow forecast, and ask if they could pay the grant earlier.
- Look at the pattern of money going out to see if anything could be paid later, for example: equipment.
- If neither is possible, approach the bank in advance, show them the cash-flow forecast, and arrange for a temporary overdraft for the period February to April.
- Also consider the possibility of temporarily investing some of the surplus money in later months.

2.7

The donor may suggest delaying the purchase of equipment, which may be possible if the whole programme is not dependent on having the equipment in place. The donor may be willing to pay grants earlier, if funds are available.

2.8

See Figure 52.

3 Records of money coming in and going out

3.1

Figure 53 *Training for Development* cash book

Date	Details	Cash amount IN	Cash amount OUT	Balance
1 Jan	Opening balance			0
1 Jan	Fees for training	1,300		1,300
4 Jan	Fees for training	2,800		4,100
4 Jan	Purchase of stationery		400	3,700
4 Jan	Purchase of desks		1,000	2,700
7 Jan	Photocopying		200	2,500
7 Jan	Purchase of training materials		900	1,600
9 Jan	Purchase of stationery		250	1,350
10 Jan	Hire of training rooms		400	950
10 Jan	Sale of booklet	25		975
14 Jan	Purchase of filing cabinet		700	275
15 Jan	Fees for training	1,350		1,625
19 Jan	Travel: Co-ordinator		320	1,305
20 Jan	Sale of materials	15		1,320
25 Jan	Purchase of small office items		240	1,080
27 Jan	Sale of booklet	25		1,105
31 Jan	**Closing balance**			**1,105**

Note: it is usual to show the balance at the beginning and end of the month. The opening balance is zero because this is a new organization.

3.2

Figure 54a

TRAINING FOR DEVELOPMENT	
	Receipt number **1**
Date *1 January*	Amount *1,300.00*
Received from	*(name of person giving cash)*
Description	*Fees for training*
Received by	*A Cashier*

Figure 54b

TRAINING FOR DEVELOPMENT	
	Receipt number **2**
Date *4 January*	Amount *2,800.00*
Received from	*(name of person giving cash)*
Description	*Fees for training*
Received by	*A Cashier*

Figure 54c

TRAINING FOR DEVELOPMENT	
	Receipt number **3**
Date *10 January*	Amount *25.00*
Received from	*(name of person giving cash)*
Description	*Fees for training*
Received by	*A Cashier*

Figure 54d

TRAINING FOR DEVELOPMENT	
	Receipt number **4**
Date *15 January*	Amount *1,350.00*
Received from	*(name of person giving cash)*
Description	*Fees for training*
Received by	*A Cashier*

Figure 54e

TRAINING FOR DEVELOPMENT	
	Receipt number **5**
Date *20 January*	Amount *15.00*
Received from *(name of person giving cash)*	
Description *Fees for training*	
Received by *A Cashier*	

Figure 54f

TRAINING FOR DEVELOPMENT	
	Receipt number **6**
Date *27 January*	Amount *25.00*
Received from *(name of person giving cash)*	
Description *Fees for training*	
Received by *A Cashier*	

Figure 55 *Training for Development* cash book (including receipt number column)

Date	Details	Receipt number	Cash amount IN	Cash amount OUT	Balance
1 Jan	Opening balance				0
1 Jan	Fees for training	1	1,300		1,300
4 Jan	Fees for training	2	2,800		4,100
4 Jan	Purchase of stationery			400	3,700
4 Jan	Purchase of desks			1,000	2,700
7 Jan	Photocopying			200	2,500
7 Jan	Purchase of training materials			900	1,600
9 Jan	Purchase of stationery			250	1,350
10 Jan	Hire of training rooms			400	950
10 Jan	Sale of booklet	3	25		975
14 Jan	Purchase of filing cabinet			700	275
15 Jan	Fees for training	4	1,350		1,625
19 Jan	Travel: Co-ordinator			320	1,305
20 Jan	Sale of materials	5	15		1,320
25 Jan	Purchase of small office items			240	1,080
27 Jan	Sale of booklet	6	25		1,105
31 Jan	**Closing balance**				**1,105**

3.3

Figure 56 *Training for Development cash book*

RECEIPTS					PAYMENTS			
Date	Details	Receipt number	Cash amount	Date	Details	Payment number	Cash amount
1 Jan	Opening balance		0	4 Jan	Purchase of stationery	P1	400
1 Jan	Fees for training	1	1,300	4 Jan	Purchase of desks	P2	1,000
4 Jan	Fees for training	2	2,800	7 Jan	Photocopying	P3	200
10 Jan	Sale of booklet	3	25	7 Jan	Purchase of training materials	P4	900
15 Jan	Fees for training	4	1,350	9 Jan	Purchase of stationery	P5	250
20 Jan	Sale of materials	5	15	10 Jan	Hire of training rooms	P6	400
27 Jan	Sale of booklet	6	25	14 Jan	Purchase of filing cabinet	P7	700
				19 Jan	Travel: Co-ordinator	P8	320
				25 Jan	Purchase of small office items	P9	240
	Total		**5,515**		**Total**		**4,410**
					Closing balance (31 January)		<u>1,105</u>

3.4

Figure 57 *Training for Development* cash counted in cash box at 31 January

	Value	multiplied by	Number	equals	Total value
Notes	20	x	11	=	220
	50	x	8	=	400
	100	x	1	=	100
Coins	1	x	33	=	33
	5	x	17	=	85
	10	x	27	=	270
Total cash counted					**1,108**
Cash book balance at 31 January					**1,105**
Difference* (if any)					**3**

*Action regarding any difference:
The cash has been recounted, and the receipts have been checked.
As this is a small amount, no action is to be taken.
A note of the difference has been made in the cash book and authorized by the group leader.

Counted by *A Cashier* **Date** 31 January **Agreed by** *A Manager* **Date** 31 January

3.5
1: b.
Reason: cash should be as secure as possible. In practice, it is better to keep the tin in a locked cupboard or safe on the premises and keep the amount of cash held to a minimum.

2: a.
Reason: the group leader needs to know as far in advance as possible if you are running out of money. This allows maximum time to try to raise more funds.

3: c.
Reason: Non-regular payments must be referred to a senior person for approval, to protect the cashier from pressure to pay. It would be sensible to make sure that the item is in the budget before making payment (option b).

4: c.
Reason: issuing receipts is a basic financial control which should always be followed.

4 Arranging your records to give more information

4.1
... type ...
... budget ... columns ...
... 'other' ...
... added up ... receipts ...
... payments ... receipts ...

4.2

Figure 58a *Training for Development analysed cash book (receipts side)*

Date	Details	Receipt number	Cash amount	Opening balance	Grants from donors	Fees for training	Sale of materials	Other receipts
1 Jan	Opening balance		0	0				
1 Jan	Fees for training	1	1,300			1,300		
4 Jan	Fees for training	2	2,800			2,800		
10 Jan	Sale of booklet	3	25				25	
15 Jan	Fees for training	4	1,350			1,350		
20 Jan	Sale of materials	5	15				15	
27 Jan	Sale of booklet	6	25				25	
	Total		**5,515**	**0**	**0**	**5,450**	**65**	**0**

Figure 58b *Training for Development analysed cash book (payments side)*

Date	Details	Payment number	Cash amount	Salaries	Rent/electricity/water/telephone	Training materials	Office expenses (including audit)	Travel/accommodation	Hire of training rooms	Office/training equipment	Other payments
4 Jan	Purchase of stationery	P1	400				400				
4 Jan	Purchase of desks	P2	1,000							1,000	
7 Jan	Photocopying	P3	200				200				
7 Jan	Purchase of training materials	P4	900			900					
9 Jan	Purchase of stationery	P5	250				250				
10 Jan	Hire of training rooms	P6	400						400		
14 Jan	Purchase of filing cabinet	P7	700							700	
19 Jan	Travel: Co-ordinator	P8	320					320			
25 Jan	Purchase of small office items	P9	240				240				
	Total		**4,410**	**0**	**0**	**900**	**1,090**	**320**	**400**	**1,700**	**0**

Closing balance (31 January) 1,105

4.3
See Figure 58a and 58b.

5 Bank accounts

5.1
See main text for details, Chapter 5.

5.2

Figure 59 Training for Development bank book

RECEIPTS				PAYMENTS				
Date	Details	Paying-in reference	Bank amount	Date	Details	Payment number	Cheque number	Bank amount
1 Jan	Opening balance		0	4 Jan	Rent	P701	406781	6,000
5 Jan	'Start-up' grant	201	25,000	7 Jan	Purchase of office chairs	P702	406782	1,750
14 Jan	Grant	202	15,000	16 Jan	Water charge	P703	406783	6,670
15 Jan	Fee for training	203	480	16 Jan	Purchase of projector and screen	P704	406784	4,800
				18 Jan	Hire of training rooms	P705	406786	890
				24 Jan	Purchase of television	P706	406787	3,000
				24 Jan	Accommodation: Co-ordinator	P707	406788	400
				31 Jan	Salaries	P708	406789	3,225
	Total		**40,480**		**Total**			**26,735**
						Closing balance (31 January)		**13,745**

5.3

Figure 60 *Training for Development* cash and bank book

	RECEIPTS						PAYMENTS				
Date	Details	Receipt number	Paying-in reference	Cash amount	Bank amount	Date	Details	Payment number	Cheque number	Cash amount	Bank amount
1 Jan	Opening balance			0	0	4 Jan	Rent	P701	406781		6,000
1 Jan	Fees for training	1		1,300		4 Jan	Purchase of stationery	P1		400	
4 Jan	Fees for training	2		2,800		4 Jan	Purchase of desks	P2		1,000	
5 Jan	'Start-up' grant	3	201		25,000	7 Jan	Photocopying	P3		200	
10 Jan	Sale of booklet			25		7 Jan	Purchase of office chairs	P702	406782		1,750
14 Jan	Grant		202		15,000	7 Jan	Purchase of training materials	P4		900	
15 Jan	Fees for training		203		480	9 Jan	Purchase of stationery	P5		250	
15 Jan	Fees for training	4		1,350		10 Jan	Hire of training rooms	P6		400	
20 Jan	Sale of materials	5		15		14 Jan	Purchase of filing cabinet	P7		700	
27 Jan	Sale of booklet	6		25		16 Jan	Water charge	P703	406783		6,670
						16 Jan	Purchase of projector and screen	P704	406784		4,800
						18 Jan	Hire of training rooms	P705	406786		890
						19 Jan	Travel: Co-ordinator	P8		320	
						24 Jan	Purchase of television	P706	406787		3,000
						24 Jan	Accommodation: Co-ordinator	P707	406788		400
						25 Jan	Purchase of small office items	P9		240	
						31 Jan	Salaries	P708	406789		3,225
	Total			**5,515**	**40,480**		**Total**			**4,410**	**26,735**
							Closing balance (31 January)			**1,105**	**13,745**

5.4

Figure 61a *Training for Development* analysed cash and bank book (receipts side)

Date	Details	Receipt number	Paying-in reference	Cash amount	Bank amount	Opening balance	Grants from donors	Fees for training	Sale of materials	Other receipts
1 Jan	Opening balance			0	0	0				
1 Jan	Fees for training	1		1,300				1,300		
4 Jan	Fees for training	2		2,800				2,800		
5 Jan	'Start-up' grant	3	201		25,000		25,000			
10 Jan	Sale of booklet	3		25					25	
14 Jan	Grant		202		15,000		15,000			
15 Jan	Fees for training		203		480			480		
15 Jan	Fees for training	4		1,350				1,350		
20 Jan	Sale of materials	5		15					15	
27 Jan	Sale of booklet	6		25					25	
	Total			5,515	40,480	0	40,000	5,930	65	0

Figure 61b Training for Development analysed cash and bank book (payments side)

Date	Details	Payment number	Cheque number	Cash amount	Bank amount	Salaries	Rent/ electricity/ water/ telephone	Training materials	Office expenses (including audit)	Travel/ accommo-dation	Hire of training rooms	Office/ training equipment	Other payments
4 Jan	Rent	P701	406781		6,000		6,000						
4 Jan	Purchase of stationery	P1		400					400				
4 Jan	Purchase of desks	P2		1,000								1,000	
7 Jan	Photocopying	P3		200					200				
7 Jan	Purchase of office chairs	P702	406782		1,750							1,750	
7 Jan	Purchase of training materials	P4		900				900					
9 Jan	Purchase of stationery	P5		250					250				
10 Jan	Hire of training rooms	P6		400							400		
14 Jan	Purchase of filing cabinet	P7		700								700	
16 Jan	Water charge	P703	406783		6,670		6,670						
16 Jan	Purchase of projector and screen	P704	406784		4,800							4,800	
18 Jan	Hire of training rooms	P705	406786		890						890		
19 Jan	Travel: Co-ordinator	P8		320						320			
24 Jan	Purchase of television	P706	406787		3,000							3,000	
24 Jan	Accommodation: Co-ordinator	P707	406788		400					400			
25 Jan	Purchase of small office items	P9		240					240				
31 Jan	Salaries	P708	406789		3,225	3,225							
	Total			4,410	26,735	3,225	12,670	900	1,090	720	1,290	11,250	0

Closing balance (31 January)   1,105   13,745

5.5

Figure 62 *Training for Development* cash and bank book

RECEIPTS						PAYMENTS					
Date	Details	Receipt number	Paying-in reference	Cash amount	Bank amount	Date	Details	Payment number	Cheque number	Cash amount	Bank amount
10 Feb	Cash to bank		210		1,200	10 Feb	Cash to bank			1,200	
12 Feb	Bank to cash			4,000		12 Feb	Bank to cash		406795		4,000

6 Making sure your figures agree with the bank's figures

6.1

- A bank statement is a list produced by a bank, showing all entries in an account over a period of time, and the balance held at the end of that period.
- A bank reconciliation is a way of confirming that a group's own accounting records agree with those of the bank.
- A bank reconciliation should be completed every time a bank statement is received or a pass book updated.
- a.   ... outstanding
  b.   ... charges ... interest ...
  c.   Tick off ...
  d.   ... table ... ticked off

6.2

The handwritten adjustments are shown in Figures 63a and 63b to explain how the bank book and bank statement are compared before the bank reconciliation statement is presented.

In addition, in this example, the bank charges are added to the bank book in January. This would often not be possible if the statement were received at a later date. In that case, the bank book would be updated in the following month, and a figure for bank charges would be added in the bank reconciliation statement in January.

Figure 63a *Training for Development* bank book as at 31 January

RECEIPTS				PAYMENTS					
Date	Details	Paying-in reference	Bank amount	Date	Details	Payment number	Cheque number	Bank amount	
1 Jan	Opening balance		0	4 Jan	Rent	P701	406781	6,000	√
5 Jan	'Start-up' grant	201	√25,000	7 Jan	Purchase of office chairs	P702	406782	1,750	√
14 Jan	Grant	202	o/s 15,000	16 Jan	Water charge	P703	406783	6,670	√
15 Jan	Fee for training	203	√ 480	16 Jan	Purchase of projector and screen	P704	406784	4,800	o/s
				18 Jan	Hire of training rooms	P705	406786	890	√
				24 Jan	Purchase of television	P706	406787	3,000	√
				24 Jan	Accommodation: Co-ordinator	P707	406788	400	o/s
				31 Jan	Salaries	P708	406789	3,225	o/s
				30 Jan	*Bank charges*			*430*	
Total			**40,480**	**Total**				**26,735**	27,165

Closing balance (31 January) ~~13,745~~ 13,315

(revised balance)

o/s = *outstanding items*

Figure 63b *Training for Development* bank statement as at 31 January

NATIONAL COMMERCIAL BANK: *Training for Development* current account				
DATE	DETAILS	IN	OUT	BALANCE
1 Jan	Opening balance			0
5 Jan	Credit	25,000 ✓		25,000
8 Jan	Cheque 406781		6,000 ✓	19,000
15 Jan	Cheque 406782		1,750 ✓	17,250
15 Jan	Credit	480 ✓		17,730
19 Jan	Cheque 406783		6,670 ✓	11,060
24 Jan	Cheque 406786		890 ✓	10,170
29 Jan	Cheque 406787		3,000 ✓	7,170
30 Jan	Bank charges ──> *update bank book*		(430)	6,740
31 Jan	**Closing balance**			**6,740**

Figure 64 *Training for Development* bank reconciliation as at 31 January

	Amount	Total amount	
Bank balance at 31 January (from bank statement)		6,740	[A]
Less: cheques not yet included in the bank's records			
cheque number 406784	4,800		
cheque number 406788	400		
cheque number 406789	3,225	8,425	[B: total cheques]
	Sub-total	(1,685)	[A–B]
Plus: items paid in but not yet included in the bank's records			
paying-in reference 202 / 14 January		15,000	[C]
Balance in bank book at 31 January (group's own record)		13,315	[A–B+C]

The amount in brackets shows that the figure is negative.

6.3
Actions

Find out what has happened to cheque 406785, which is missing in the sequence. If it has been cancelled, it should be retained in the cheque book and clearly marked 'cancelled'.

Ask the bank why the grant of 15,000.00 has not been credited to the account on 14 January. How was *Training for Development* notified? Did the bank charges result because this amount is not in the account? If so, could a refund be claimed?

6.4

The handwritten adjustments are shown in Figures 65a and 65b to explain how the bank book and bank statement are compared before the bank reconciliation statement is presented.

Figure 65a *Northern Agricultural Programme* bank book

RECEIPTS

Date	Details	Paying-in reference	Bank amount
1 May	Opening balance		5,205
9 May	Transfer from deposit account	–	✓ 5,000
29 May	Amount received from PNY	156	o/s 3,497
23 May	*Interest (received)*	–	145 o/s
Total			~~13,702~~

13,847

PAYMENTS

Date	Details	Payment number	Cheque number	Bank amount	
4 May	Bank to cash	P1003	4017	250	✓
7 May	Rent (1 Jan to 30 June)	P1004	4019	4,754	✓
12 May	Repairs	P1005	4020	601	✓
19 May	Telephone	P1006	4021	143	o/s
23 May	Bank charges	–	–	58	✓
28 May	Bank to cash	P1007	4022	300	✓
28 May	Salaries	P1008	4023	4,167	o/s
28 May	Tax payment	P1009	4024	1,305	o/s
28 May	Pension payment	P1010	4025	280	o/s
Total				**11,858**	

Closing balance (31 May)   ~~1,844~~

1,989

(revised balance)

o/s = *outstanding items*

Figure 65b *Northern Agricultural Programme* bank statement

STANDARD BANK: *Northern Agricultural Programme* current account					
DATE	**DETAILS**		**IN**	**OUT**	**BALANCE**
1 May	Opening balance				7,764
2 May	Cheque 4015	*Relate to April*		195	7,569
6 May	Cheque 4016	*bank book*		2,364	5,205
10 May	Cheque 4017			250 ✓	4,955
10 May	Cheque 4019			4,754 ✓	201
17 May	Cheque 4020			601 ✓	400 OD
23 May	Interest ⟶ *update bank book*	(145)			255 OD
23 May	Transfer		5,000 ✓		4,745
23 May	Charges			58 ✓	4,687
28 May	Cheque 4022			300 ✓	4,387
31 May	**Closing balance**				**4,387**
OD = overdrawn amount					

Figure 66 *Northern Agricultural Programme* bank reconciliation statement at 31 May

	Amount	Total amount	
Bank balance at 31 May (from bank statement)		4,387	[A]
Less: cheques not yet included in the bank's records			
cheque number 4021	143		
cheque number 4023	4,167		
cheque number 4024	1,305		
cheque number 4025	280	5,895	[B: total cheques]
	Sub-total	(1,508)	[A–B]
Plus: items paid in but not yet included in the bank's records			
paying-in reference 156 / 29 May		3,497	[C]
Balance in bank book at 31 May (group's own record)		1,989	[A–B+C]

6.5
Questions to ask include:

- Why did the transfer from the deposit account go through the bank book on 9 May but not appear on the bank statement until 23 May?
- Where is cheque number 4018? Has it been cancelled?
- What is the reason for the bank charges? How have they been calculated?
- Is it possible to negotiate payment of rent every three months?

6.6
1: d.
Reason: any bank accounts should be opened in the name of the group.

2: c.
Reason: to avoid errors or theft.

3: b.
Reason: generally improves security.

4: a.
Reason: tightens financial control and is good practice.

7 Summarizing the accounts

7.1

Figure 67 *Training for Development* receipts and payments account (receipts side)

RECEIPTS	Amount	Total amount
Opening balance bank/cash, 1 January		0
Grants from donors	40,000	
Fees for training	5,930	
Sale of materials	65	
Other receipts	0	
Total receipts		45,995

7.2

Figure 68 *Training for Development* receipts and payments account (payments side)

PAYMENTS	Amount	Total amount
Salaries	3,225	
Rent	6,000	
Electricity/water/telephone	6,670	
Training materials	900	
Office expenses (including audit)	1,090	
Travel and accommodation	720	
Hire of training rooms	1,290	
Office equipment	3,450	
Training equipment	7,800	
Other payments	0	
Total payments		31,145
Closing balance, 31 January		**14,850**

7.3

Figure 69 *Training for Development* receipts and payments account for the period 1–31 January

	Amount	Total amount	
RECEIPTS			
Opening balance, 1 January		0	[A]
Grants from donors	40,000		
Fees for training	5,930		
Sale of materials	65		
Other receipts	0		
Total receipts		45,995	[B]
		45,995	[A+B]
PAYMENTS			
Salaries	3,225		
Rent	6,000		
Electricity/water/telephone	6,670		
Training materials	900		
Office expenses, including audit	1,090		
Travel/accommodation	720		
Hire of training rooms	1,290		
Office equipment	3,450		
Training equipment	7,800		
Other payments	0		
Total payments		31,145	[C]
Closing balance bank/cash, 31 January		**14,850**	[A+B–C]

[The letters A, B and C are included to show where the calculations are made. These would not usually be included in a receipts and payments account.]

8 Summarizing the accounts with more information

8.1

a. **Limitation:**

The receipts and payments account does not state how much relates to a specific period of time. For example, if rent is paid for 15 months it will be included, regardless of the fact that the account is merely for 12 months.

How to overcome:

- Keeping outstanding amounts to a minimum at the date when the receipts and payments account will be prepared.
- Keep a record of outstanding items and include as a note at the bottom of the receipts and payments account.

b. **Limitation:**

Long-term and short-term items are treated in the same way.

How to overcome:

- Add a note of 'fixed assets' at the bottom of the receipts and payments account.

c. **Limitation:**

A surplus (profit) or deficit (loss) figure is not shown at the end of the period. The receipts and payments account only shows the cash and bank balance at this date.

How to overcome:

- Notes added to the account will show outstanding commitments.
- If it is essential to have details of surplus or deficit figures, help should be sought from an accountant.

8.2

Money should be put aside regularly in a savings or deposit account to replace 'fixed assets'.

9 Providing the information your group needs

9.1

Figure 70 *Training for Development* budget and actual statement for the month of January

Item	Note	Budgeted amount for January	Amount received/spent in January	Difference
RECEIPTS				
Dept of Education 'start-up' grant		25,000	25,000	0
Grants received from donors		15,000	15,000	0
Fees for training		5,500	5,930	430
Sale of materials		100	65	(35)
Total receipts		**45,600**	**45,995**	**395**
PAYMENTS				
Salaries		3,750	3,225	525
Office rent		6,000	6,000	0
Electricity/water/telephone		7,000	6,670	330
Training materials		500	900	(400)
Office expenses, including audit		750	1,090	(340)
Travel and accommodation		1,500	720	780
Hire of training rooms		1,750	1,290	460
Office equipment		13,000	3,450	9,550
Training equipment		11,000	7,800	3,200
Total payments		**45,250**	**31,145**	**14,105**
Total difference		**350**	**14,850**	**14,500**

9.2
This is because the negative difference indicates an under-collection of budgeted receipts but an overspend on payments (rather than an underspend). The brackets help to show the areas where we need to concentrate our efforts: where receipts have not arrived or there is overspending.

9.3
If an entry for 'transfer to a savings account' had been made, a figure would have been shown in the 'amount received/ spent' column of the payments section of the statement in Activity 9.1. A note would be added at the bottom of the table to explain this.

9.4
Notes

1. Office and training equipment represents fixed assets bought during January	
Office	**Cost**
Desks	1,000
Office chairs	1,750
Filing cabinet	700
Total office equipment	**3,450**
Training	**Cost**
Projector and screen	4,800
Television	3,000
Total training equipment	**7,800**
2. Amounts held in cash and bank	
Balance held in cash, 31 January	1,105
Balance in current account, 31 January	13,745
Total	**14,850**

9.5
Questions include:

- Salaries can usually be accurately calculated in the budget. Why were they less than estimated?
- Why are the training materials and office expenses greater than estimated?
- Why are travel/accommodation and hire of training rooms under budget?
  (Remember that the receipts and payments account is not always an accurate comparison with the budget, because payments in advance and in arrears are not adjusted. This may be the answer.)
- Is there more office equipment and training equipment still to be purchased? If so, for what amount?
- If there is no money set aside for the replacement of the fixed assets already purchased, how will they be replaced?

The management committee may also wish to see a copy of the revised cash-flow forecast, along with the budget and actual statement.

10 Having the accounts checked

10.1
Independence

10.2
- cash and bank books;
- receipts for money coming in and payments going out;
- invoices;
- information from donors;
- any correspondence about the group, and especially about the accounting;
- bank statements or pass books;
- cheque books and old cheque 'stubs', paying-in slips/books;
- bank reconciliations, especially for the year-end;
- budget and actual statements;
- receipts and payments account;
- a record of any group meetings.

10.3
A management letter suggests ways for a group to improve its internal organization and make its activities more effective.

10.4
Points to include:

- No one outside the group looks at the accounting, and there is a lack of transparency. The group may not be seen to be honest.
- Valuable advice from an examiner/auditor is not available to the group.
- The group lacks the credibility that an examination/audit provides.
- Donors may refuse to fund the group.

11 Relations with donors

11.1
   ... high standard of accounting ...
   ... the types of programme that they are likely to fund
   ... keep the donor informed
   ... kept carefully

11.2
1: b.
Reason: donors will wish to see that you have contacted a range of suppliers to find the best value. Donors may also ask for some of the other options!

2: d.
Reason: accounting staff have to prepare additional budgets and report on financial activities to donors.

3: a.
Reason: the letter of agreement will give details of reports required and their frequency.

12 Regular financial tasks

12.1
See the text in Chapter 12 for details.

Resources

Written resources
Accounting topics

John Cammack (2000) *Financial Management for Development: Accounting and Finance for the Non-Specialist in Development Organizations*, Oxford: International NGO Training and Research Centre (INTRAC).

K.N. Gupta (2004) *Manual of Financial Management and Legal Regulations*, Delhi: Financial Management Services Foundation.

International Labour Office (1999) *Improve Your Business Handbook*, (international edn), Geneva: International Labour Office. Also *Improve Your Business Trainer's Guide*.

M. Kandasami (1998) *Governance and Financial Management in Non-Profit Organizations*, New Delhi: Caritas India.

Capacity building and financial communication

John Cammack (2012) *Communicating Financial Management with Non-finance People: A Manual for International Development Workers*, Rugby, UK: Practical Action Publishing.

John Cammack (2014) *Building Financial Management Capacity for NGOs and Community Organizations: A Practical Guide*, Rugby, UK: Practical Action Publishing.

Anthony Davies (1997) *Managing for Change: How to Run Community Development Projects*, Rugby, UK: Practical Action Publishing in association with Voluntary Service Overseas.

Training topics

Robert Chambers (2002) *Participatory Workshops*, London: Earthscan.

Irene Guijt, Jules N. Pretty, Ian Scoones, and John Thompson (1995) *Participatory Learning and Action – A Trainer's Guide*, London: International Institute of Environment and Development.

Web resources

Accounting

www.bond.org.uk (click on 'resources'/search keywords 'how to')
Bond 'How to ...' guides on project budgeting and other topics.
www.civicus.org (click on 'resources'/'toolkits')
Civicus 'toolkits' include finance and fundraising topics.
www.fme-online.org
Financial Management for Emergencies provide good practice and examples of formats for accounting in development organizations as well as emergencies.
www.johncammack.net (click on 'links' and 'resources')
Links to sites about accounting and financial management, and downloadable computer spreadsheet templates for budgeting and cash-flow forecasting.
www.mango.org.uk
Accounting and financial resources.
www.ncvo-vol.org.uk (click on 'practical support'/'financial management' and 'funding')
Resources about financial management and financing organizations.
www.ngomanager.org (click on 'library'/'e-library')
Resources on managing finance and funding.
www.practicalactionpublishing.org
Some materials and activities from this book are available to download.

Training

www.aidsalliance.org (click on 'resources'/'key resources')
Guide on '100 ways to energize groups: games to use in workshops, meetings and the community'.
www.ica-sae.org (click on 'publication'/'Training the Trainer resource pack')
International Council on Archives; Training the Trainer resource pack.
www.trainingzone.co.uk
Tips on a range of training topics.